GEORGE STRAIT

For years, he kicked around small-town barrooms, smoke-filled dancehalls, and cheap Texas honky-tonks, crooning the Hank Williams songbook with all his heart and strumming away on his guitar for free beer and pretzels. He knew Nashville was a distant dream. But he wouldn't give up. George Strait was going to become a country music star—and nothing on this sweet earth was going to stop him.

COUNTRY MUSIC'S LIVING LEGEND

- More Number One hits than any other male country music star
- Winner ASCAP's Voice of Music Award
- Multiple winner of the Country Music Association Awards for Best Single of the Year, Best Album of the Year and Best Male Vocalist of the Year.
- Broke Elvis Presley's record for the most sold-out performances at the Las Vegas Hilton

<u>BOOK YOUR PLACE ON OUR WEBSITE</u> AND MAKE THE <u>READING CONNECTION!</u>

We've created a customized website just for our very special readers, where you can get the inside scoop on everything that's going on with Zebra, Pinnacle and Kensington books.

When you come online, you'll have the exciting opportunity to:

- View covers of upcoming books
- Read sample chapters
- Learn about our future publishing schedule (listed by publication month *and author*)
- Find out when your favorite authors will be visiting a city near you
- Search for and order backlist books from our online catalog
- Check out author bios and background information
- Send e-mail to your favorite authors
- Meet the Kensington staff online
- Join us in weekly chats with authors, readers and other guests
- Get writing guidelines
- AND MUCH MORE!

**Visit our website at
http://www.pinnaclebooks.com**

The Story of Country's Living Legend

GEORGE STRAIT

MARK BEGO

P

Pinnacle Books
Kensington Publishing Corp.

http://www.pinnaclebooks.com

PINNACLE BOOKS are published by

Kensington Publishing Corp.
850 Third Avenue
New York, NY 10022

Pinnacle and the P logo Reg. U.S. Pat. & TM Off.

First Kensington Hardcover Printing: January, 1997
First Pinnacle Printing: March, 1999
10 9 8 7 6 5 4 3 2 1

Printed in the United States of America

To Brad Demeulenaere:

You, along with your sister Kara, and your friend Brendan Thompson, have been so helpful in lending me your clipping and photo files, on so many great stars . . . including George Strait . . .

Thank you for being such a wonderful and devoted friend!

Acknowledgments:

The Arizona Daily Star
Mary & Bob Bego
Angela Bowie
Chevrolet Motor Company
David Daily
Marie Dillon
Brad DeMeulenaere
Kara DeMeulenaere
Paul Dinas
Gino Falzarano
Karen Haas
Simone Lazer
Jim Lauderdale
Mick Lloyd
Virginia Lohle
Marcy MacDonald
Sindi Markoff
Toni Mason
Christi McCoy
John McCoy
George Plentzas
Marisa Redanty
Tony Seidl
Shooting Star Photos
Troy Sniff
Mark Sokoloff
Brendan Thompson
Mary Wilson

Contents

Introduction
by Jim Lauderdale

The first time I met George Strait, was at the premiere of his film, *Pure Country*, in 1993. His recording two of my songs as part of the soundtrack for that film was the beginning of our professional friendship. I feel like I owe George so much, because of his recording "Where the Sidewalk Ends" and "The King of Broken Hearts," and all of the subsequent songs of mine that he has recorded for the next four albums. It really was a turning point in my writing career.

On the last day of the final soundtrack recording session for *Pure Country*, his producer, Tony Brown, played "Where the Sidewalk Ends" and "The King of Broken Hearts," and they ended up cutting them both for the film. I found out about it just a couple of days later, and I just couldn't believe the good news. When the movie finally premiered in Nashville, I went with Renee Bell, who worked at MCA Records at the time. That evening was so great for me. I was surprised when I saw the final cut of the movie that evening. I knew they were going to use "When the Sidewalk

Ends" as part of George's character's last set, but they kept playing it over and over again. It was just such a huge thrill to be sitting there hearing my song coming from the movie screen! It was just a wonderful feeling.

I was introduced to George Strait at the party afterwards. He was so warm, and so down-to-earth and friendly, I could tell that he was really a special person. He's just got such a real easy-going magnetism about him.

The next time I saw him was while he was working on his next album. I was pitching songs to him, but nothing was sticking for the sessions. I took him a couple of more songs, kinda at the last minute, while he and Tony were already in the studio recording, and they ended up on the record. I am happy to say, that George has been using my songs on every one of his albums ever since. Right now I'm working on some new songs for his 1997 album, in hopes that they will be included!

I just recorded a new album of my songs called *Persimmons* for Upstart Records, and I am about to launch my very own country recording career on RCA in the next couple of months. However, writing some new songs for George Strait is among my top concerns. He is one of the major stars I write for—if not *the* major star whom I write for. His recording my songs really catapulted my career into the fast lane. And then, for him to keep on recording my songs, album after album, has really put me on the map in Nashville.

Three years after its release, the *Pure Country* soundtrack is still on the *Billboard* magazine Country Album chart. It has sold over five million copies and it is still in the Top 75. Every once in a while it will come up or down several points on the chart, but, to-date, it is still hanging in there. That album was a great boost for me. George's boxed set, *Strait Out of the Box,* which my songs are also on, is the biggest selling multiple-CD package in country history, outselling even *The Patsy Cline Collection.* Believe me, I am pulling out all of the stops to have one of my songs on his next album as well!

What is it about George Strait that gives him such lasting appeal and longevity over the past 16 years? It is a hard question to answer, but I can honestly say, there is just something about him, some undefinable quality about him that makes people love him. He's got millions of devoted fans. A lot of people come and go in country music, but he is just very consistent, and selling better than ever! One of the main keys to his success, is years of making great records, and putting on really great live shows.

I remember the first time I saw George Strait perform in concert was in 1981 or 1982. It was at a country music club on Fifth Avenue and 13th Street in New York City, called The Lone Star Cafe. I was just blown away by him and his music. Here was a guy that was doing Western swing music. The group Asleep at the Wheel, were probably the only other people who were doing that at the time on a major label. The mixture of Western swing music, and the kind of Merle Haggard-esque material that he was doing, was just a knock-out punch. It was a great combination of sounds which he started out doing, and is continuing into the 1990s.

What is it that makes people gravitate towards George and his music year after year? I think that it is because he is *real*. He is a devoted family man, and he just seems like such a down-to-earth person as a human being. Success has not ruined him. He is living the good life, and he is happy, and I think that people pick up on that genuineness. I can speak from experience when I say that he is as warm and friendly and genuine as he looks up there on stage, on television, and on record: that *is* the real George Strait!

—September 1996

Chapter One

"Meet George Strait"

There is a point in the 1993 film *Pure Country* where George Strait all of a sudden just "clicks" on screen, as a believable modern day, all-American hero. Instantly, all doubts or questions about the reason for his enduring appeal suddenly vanish, and it all comes clear. The key to his success is that he is just a plain "likable" guy, with a warm personality and winning style.

In the film, Strait portrays fictional country/rock singer Dusty, who is running away from the life that his career has forced him into. The film gave millions of people a taste of the simple charm and undeniable class that country music fans have known about for two decades now.

In my mind, the scene that really cements it is the one mid-film where George is discussing with his costar, Isabel Glasser, the drunken barroom brawl that had taken place the previous evening. The scene begins with George standing in the backlit doorway of a barn somewhere on a ranch in the western part of middle America. The dialogue is shot through a yellow-colored lens to give it the look of a country setting at sunrise. The only background music is the clucking of a couple of chickens and the sounds of a horse's heavy breathing.

George is wearing one of his trademark white straw cowboy hats, a pair of well-worn jeans and a long-sleeved, cowboy-cut, button-down Western shirt. As the brief scene unfolds, George and Isabel progress to brushing one of the horses in the barn. As they speak to each other, there is an unassuming and very natural tone to Strait's voice, something very genuine and friendly. Right then and there, as the yellow light plays off his face, some sort of magical sparkle comes through his intense and honest hazel eyes.

It isn't that what he has to say is so brilliant, or that he looks "hot" in a muscular "beefcake" sort of way—it's his humble yet attractive magnetism that shines through. Women find him sexy, and men seem to sense a genuine honesty that makes him seem like everybody's best buddy.

In a way, that one brief scene, which lasts less than five minutes, truly crystallizes what it is that makes George Strait a star. Like the character Dusty he portrays in the film, it is not the smoke, the lights, or the special effects that make him such an entertaining star. Like alchemy, chemistry, or even a good recipe, somehow something magical comes together in the voice, the look, and the image of George Strait.

With all of that said, yes, he does have a certain star quality. However, that still doesn't explain the amazing career longevity. What is it that makes George Strait so popular year after year? What sets him apart from the other stars at the top of the country charts?

Garth Brooks, Wynonna, Billy Ray Cyrus, Alan Jackson, and even Patsy Cline all have bigger-selling single albums than he does. Although George has an impressive collection of awards, he hardly has the most. With his straight-forward and smooth vocal style, he does not have the most dramatic or immediately recognizable voice in Nashville either.

So, what is the reason for his being the most consistent and the longest lasting male superstar in 1990s country music? Is it his looks? His voice? Or the fact that in a decade that is decidedly "all frills," George Strait remains absolutely "no frills"?

If you attend a Garth Brooks, Reba McEntire, or Brooks & Dunn concert, you know you're going to get over an hour of bells and whistles, smoke and lights. If you go to a George Strait concert, you're going to get good solid music, simply delivered by a man who just stands there and sings—no choreography, no pyrotechnics, and no costume changes.

While he initially took a ton of flak for wearing a cowboy hat—as modern country's first "hat act"—he wears it not as a stage prop or a costume for effect, but because he *is* a real-life cowboy. When he isn't onstage entertaining thousands of cheering fans, he can be found on his Texas ranch, roping cattle and ridin' the range.

What is fascinating about country singing star George Strait is not that he has racked up more Number One hits than anyone in the 1990s country music scene, or that he is the first "new traditionalist" country singing sensation to become a movie star, but the fact that he continues to keep his career hot after sixteen years at the top. He never has had a scorching, impossible-to-follow hit like Billy Ray Cyrus, nor does he suddenly and dramatically announce that he is quitting the business like Garth Brooks, nor will you find him rocking out on a Grateful Dead tribute album like Dwight Yoakam. The way in which he has achieved his goals is also important. He has his own pure and simple formula for his life and for his career, and it has rewarded him again and again.

George arrived on the 1980s post-*Urban Cowboy* country music scene around the same time that Rosanne Cash,

Alabama, Ricky Skaggs, Randy Travis and Reba McEntire were all making names for themselves in Nashville. When the current new wave of country popularity skyrocketed in the 1990s, Strait was simply swept up in it, and this new country tidal wave has provided him with some of his biggest successes.

The bedrock of his career is his incredible string of more than thirty Number One hits. With it, George holds the record for the longest-spanning list of chart-topping singles in modern country music. George's smashes include "Unwound" in 1981, "Amarillo by Morning," "Ocean Front Property," "All My Ex's Live in Texas," "Marina Del Rey," "Nobody in His Right Mind Would've Left Her," "Heartland," "Easy Come, Easy Go," right up to "Check Yes or No" in 1996. In addition, his plain and simple good looks have been celebrated in one of *People* magazine's recent lists of the "50 Most Beautiful People in the World."

Never one to rest on his laurels, his latest album, 1996's *Blue Clear Sky,* entered the charts at Number One in *Billboard* magazine. George's impressive 1995 career retrospective four-CD boxed set, *Strait Out of the Box,* has the distinction of becoming the best-selling boxed compilation in the history of country music. What is it that fuels George Strait's steady and consistent drive to succeed? To answer that question, one has to go all the way back to his childhood, and his roots.

A native Texan, George Strait has always been a man of two main passions: country music and rodeo riding. Like Roy Rogers and Gene Autry before him, he grew up with strong images of singing cowboys. Happily for him, he has been able to combine these interests into a successful career. The singing, the cowboy hats, and the romance of riding his horse around his own ranch are not just images for George Strait; they are his reality, his background, his heritage.

His life has been *almost* storybook perfect. He came from

a solid Texas background: his father was a rancher and school teacher; his mother, a homemaker. He courted and married his longtime high school sweetheart, Norma, and after he graduated from college, he joined the army.

It was while stationed in Hawaii that he really began exploring the world of music. George was able to teach himself how to play the guitar, picking favorite tunes out of a Hank Williams, Sr., songbook. After the army, he returned to Texas, received his bachelor's degree in agriculture, and in 1975 formed his own band, Ace in the Hole. While he continued to chase after his dreams of a musical career, George and Norma set up housekeeping in Texas ranch country and raised a family.

After five years of kicking around in barrooms and dance halls, George began to wonder whether his visions of musical success were nothing more than dreams out of the clear blue sky. Through a fortunate chain of events, eventually, his lucky break came around. With the help of his devoted career-long manager, Erv Woolsey, in 1981 George released his debut album, *Strait Country.* He followed it up with *Strait from the Heart* (1982), and *Right or Wrong* (1983). In 1983, another of George's dreams came true when he organized and hosted his first annual rodeo fest: "The George Strait Team Roping Classic." It is held every June in Kingsville, Texas.

In 1985 he released his first Greatest Hits album, and when his 1986 album, *Ocean Front Property,* was released, it made music history by debuting on the *Billboard* country music chart at Number One.

While his career has been one long string of impressive concert and music chart successes, George Strait's life has not been without its tragedies. In 1986 his thirteen-year-old daughter was killed in a car accident. He refused all press interviews after that—unable to discuss this horrifying loss with perfect strangers. To work his way through his pain, George completely immersed himself in his career. He had no alternative but to continue to live his life in his own signature fashion.

From 1986 to 1990, he continued to produce the kind of country music that he loved, including the exciting *Beyond the Blue Neon*. When the 1990s ushered in a whole new genre of country stars like Garth Brooks, Alan Jackson, and Clint Black, George found that they all listed him as one of their greatest influences. Instead of making Strait seem like the star of a bygone era, they helped keep the spotlight on him, his concerts, and his records.

In 1992 the opportunity for George to star in the film *Pure Country* with Lesley Ann Warren came along. Now he wasn't just going to emulate the cinema cowboys of his youth—he was going to become one of them. He jumped into the project with both feet. Not only did the movie become a Top Ten box-office hit, but the film's soundtrack provided George with his seventeenth Gold album. With sales in excess of five million copies sold, it is the largest selling album of his career.

George Strait has been considered by country music fan magazines as a reigning "Country Hunk" for over a dozen years now. He is still a hit with his old fans from the 1980s, as well as having accrued millions more listeners in the 1990s. George has an infallible knack for being in the right place at the right time, and sitting on the top of the country charts has very comfortably become like home to him.

In the biographies and autobiographies of most modern singing stars, the readers find themselves careening from one highly publicized scandal to the next. All too often, displays of wild behavior become the guideposts for their lives and their careers. Not so with George Strait. The deep dark secret to his winning success is that there *is* no secret. While writing this book, I tried valiantly to discover all of the hidden kinks and twists in ultra-straight George Strait. There are none! In the show business realm, this is the exception, and not the rule. This is only one of the many facts that make George Strait so refreshingly different!

In recent years hit country star autobiographies have become quite popular, as witnessed by the best-sellers penned by Dolly Parton, Reba McEntire, Naomi Judd, George Jones, and Travis Tritt. In 1996, when George Strait was asked about writing his own autobiography, he replied, "I've been asked about doing a book for a long time. I don't really have any desire to do one right now. But I think maybe later on, it might be something that would be neat to do. We've had some interesting things happen. But not in the near future. I'm talking later, years down the road. So, who knows: *Strait out of the Book!* I think I've done enough 'Strait' stuff!"[1]

For that very reason, this book provides the first—and thus far only—book to fully compile, present and examine the life and the creative artistry of the man who is the forerunner and the backbone of today's country music. There is only one George Strait—and this is his story.

Chapter Two

"Strait Texas"

If you travel about twenty-five miles due south of San Antonio, on Highway 16, you'll run into the small town of Poteet, Texas. Locally, Poteet is known as "The Strawberry Capital of the World." It was there that George Strait was born on May 18, 1952. Both George and his older brother, Buddy, were raised by their parents in nearby Pearsall. George's father, John Strait, taught mathematics at a local junior high school, and his mother was a homemaker.

George and Buddy were exposed to horseback riding and cattle roping at an early age. Weekends were spent at their grandparents' two thousand acre ranch located in Big Wells, about forty miles southwest of Pearsall. When George was in fourth grade, his mother and father divorced. In all of his press biographies, mention of his mother is conspicuously missing. All that George will mention to this day is that she left the family, his parents divorced, and she was no longer actively in their lives. From that point forward, and throughout their entire childhood, John Strait centered his life on raising his young sons.

Speaking of his father, George explains, "He just dedicated the rest of his whole life to raising my brother and me. And he very seldom even dated. He taught school and worked on the ranch. It was only after Buddy and I got out of the house that he cut loose and started having some fun again, and eventually remarried."[2]

Many performers look back and see their lives as the product of households that were filled with music as they grew up, and acknowledge how they drew upon that for inspiration. George's homelife couldn't have been any farther from that. "My dad didn't even have a record player," George recalls, "and when he listened to the radio, it was usually the news or the cow market reports, or something like that. If a song happened to come on, I never paid much attention to what it was."[3]

In addition to school and ranching, religion also played a strong part in shaping young George. He never really sat around and daydreamed about what he wanted to be when he grew up. He just assumed that he'd figure all of that out when the time was right. According to him, "My dad, of course, raised my brother and me on his own, and he raised us in a real religious atmosphere. We're all Baptists, and he always told me that the Lord would tell me what he wanted me to do with my life; and I kind of believe that's really true. So I didn't worry about it much, didn't think about it that much."[4]

It wasn't until he was a teenager that he finally became exposed to popular music. "I was interested in music in high school," George remembers, "but it was more rock & roll. I mean, The Beatles were big then, so I was listening a lot to them, and to a lot of other pop music at the time. I started getting interested in country music shortly after my senior year in high school. I totally got into the music of Merle Haggard, George Jones, and Bob Wills & His Texas Playboys. Those were *it!* That's really about all I listened to. Merle, George and Bob Wills, man! And once I got interested in country, I just fell in love with it."[5]

While he was still in school, he met and fell in love with Norma, one of his classmates. She was quite literally his high school sweetheart. George admits that at that age he wasn't much for paying attention to his studies and didn't make very good grades in school.

Right after he graduated from Pearsall High School, George and Norma drove south to Mexico and were married. Their parents were so dismayed that they had eloped, that the young couple was convinced to hold a small church wedding for family and friends, to make it really official.

There are two cities on Highway I-35 between San Antonio and Austin. Both of these towns were to become instrumental in the development of George Strait's musical career. In the fall of 1970, George enrolled in college, at Southwest Texas State University in San Marcos. He spent three semesters there before suddenly deciding to join the army in late 1971. The Vietnam War was in full swing, and George was stationed in the middle of the Pacific Ocean in Hawaii.

Norma moved to Hawaii to be with George for the three years he was stationed there. George's post was in the payroll department of the base. To entertain himself, on a lark, one day in 1972, George got the idea in his head that he wanted to dabble a bit in music. As he explains it, "I went out and bought an old cheap guitar. It was all I could afford at the time, and some old Hank Williams songbooks, and I started teaching myself to play the guitar."[6] Armed with a bunch of songbooks which had small charts showing where to put your fingers, he proceeded to pick his way to proficiency.

Not content to just play "Your Cheatin' Heart" at a beer bash at the barracks, George decided that he would like to learn enough songs to start playing in the local clubs. It wasn't long before he put together his own band, and did just that. George's first band only stayed together for two months before breaking up, but that was all that he needed to get a taste of what it was like to deliver a song from onstage. It proved infectious for the twenty-year-old Strait.

The following year, it came to George's attention that the commanding officer was holding auditions for musical groups to entertain at functions on the base. He was going to put together four different groups, each one proficient in either Hawaiian, R&B, rock & roll, or country. Strait not only auditioned, but he became the lead singer of the country ensemble. During his last year in the army he didn't have to wear army clothes. He spent his time entertaining the base with country music in Western clothes.

It was in Hawaii that George began always wearing a cowboy hat onstage. It was to become his trademark.

As the lead singer of the army base country party band, George had found his niche. It somehow unleashed a different side of his personality. He loved holding the attention of the audience in his grasp while he performed. "I always knew I wanted to be a country singer," he explained. "But it wasn't until I ended up in Hawaii that I really got serious about it."[7] He sent off for sheet music by artists like Hank Williams, George Jones and Merle Haggard, who George acknowledges are still his biggest influences.

It got to the point where launching a career in country music was all that he could talk or think about. He would dream about a music career, sometimes lying awake with Norma and imagining how it could be.

George began seeking out country albums in his search for fresh material. It was a 1970 Merle Haggard LP that was destined to open up a whole new world of music for him. The recording was Haggard's version of the hits of Bob Wills & His Texas Playboys. This was George's first introduction to Western swing music.

"Merle Haggard, he kind of led me along," Strait

recalled. "He grabbed me with his music and jerked me into Bob Wills. His album, *The Best Damn Fiddle Player in the World,* was *the* album for me. It's such a great album. Him and Wills go together for me. Merle's the one that got me into swing. It opened up a whole new deal for me. I tell ya, we used to do so much swing we probably used to make people sick. They were like, 'Hey, play something else.' "[8]

During all of those years growing up in Texas, George Strait never had a musical idol to fuel his creative dreams and make him want to devote his life to making music. He was twenty years old when he discovered the music of Bob Wills & His Texas Playboys. Throughout his entire musical career, it has been Wills whom Strait most admired, and the influence of Wills and the songs he made famous have consistently inspired him.

Since Bob Wills had such an impact on the life of George Strait, it is important to know a little bit about the life and times of the one and only king of Western swing. Born in 1905 in Kosse, Texas, James Robert Wills came from a family of fiddlers. His grandfathers on both sides of the family were master fiddlers, as well as five of his aunts and nine of his uncles. If anyone was born to play the country fiddle, it was Bob. He was able to play both the mandolin and the guitar behind his father at local parties and get-togethers.

Bob came from a dirt-poor family in the panhandle of Texas, and they picked cotton alongside several black families in the same financial straits. From them he learned elements of the traditional blues. At the age of twenty, he had migrated to the seven-year-old state of New Mexico. While there, he played music with several local Mexican musicians. From them he picked up the flavor of traditional Mexican music which inspired his first composition, "Spanish Two-Step."

In 1929, Bob was playing the fiddle and singing and

dancing in an actual Medicine Show. From that experience, he gleaned a certain sense of hokey vaudeville. That same year he returned to Texas, where he landed a job at a Fort Worth radio station, working in the studio band.

Bob put together his first group of Texas Playboys in Tulsa, Oklahoma, in the early 1930s. From 1934, Bob and His Texas Playboys continued to blend elements of jazz, big band swing, country/western cowboy music, the fiddles of Appalachian folk/country, and Mexican *corridos* (story songs). Bob was quite a character. He would shout out commands to his band in the middle of a tune, signaling different soloists' turns. In 1935 the band began their recording career and very quickly gathered a devoted following. They were unlike anyone in the business, and for the next forty years Bob Wills was a bona fide country star and a living legend with country music lovers.

It was Bob Wills who first brought cowboy hats, bolo ties, and cowboy boots into Nashville, and made that fashion statement all the rage with country musicians in Music City. According to Ray Benson of the group Asleep at the Wheel, "After Bob Wills played the Grand Ole Opry in 1940, every hillbilly band got rid of their overalls and flannel shirts and got cowboy hats and Western suits!"[9]

In 1940 Bob Wills & His Texas Playboys moved out to Hollywood, where they were featured in over a dozen low budget western films. When the Second World War ended, Wills and his eighteen-piece band were frequent attractions in the budding gambling town of Las Vegas. He became famous for his songs including "Ida Red," "Lily Dale," "Deep Water," "Milk Cow Blues," "Blues for Dixie," "Misery," "Faded Love," "Corina, Corina," "Across the Alley From the Alamo," "Stay a Little Longer," and "Right or Wrong."

When Bob Wills died in 1975 he left behind him a legacy of incredible music. His tunes have been revived time and time again—from Patsy Cline's heart-wrenching 1960 version of "Faded Love," to Joni Mitchell's 1988 arrangement of "Corina, Corina." Asleep at the Wheel's star-studded Bob Wills tribute album in 1993 proved George Strait wasn't the only person in the 1970s who discovered and went crazy about the music of Bob Wills & His Texas Play-boys. Ray Benson, the driving force behind Asleep at the Wheel, was also mesmerized by Wills' timeless tunes.

Although he was inspired by the music of Bob Wills, George didn't harbor any daydreams of musical stardom; he just knew that music was something he enjoyed creating.

In 1974, after three years in Hawaii in the army, George and Norma returned to Texas. George returned to college at Southwest Texas State University. He was able to go to school on the GI Bill, which gave him some extra money to get his degree *and* play music—everything he wanted to do. He had decided to pursue country music as a career, and the GI Bill gave him the opportunity to do it.

Actually, George was juggling dreams of his two passions: rodeo riding and singing. The singing initially won the career tug-of-war. "I would have loved to have been a professional rodeo roper," George still proclaims. "But when it came time for me to choose a career, Norma and I had just gotten married, and country music seemed to have a better future. Looking back, I guess that I made the right decision, but rodeo will always be an important part of my life. There are team-roping events put on just for guys in their fifties and sixties, so I'll be able to do this for a long time."[10]

He studied for his degree in Agricultural Science by day, and at night he was the leader of the very first incarnation of the Ace in the Hole band, founded in 1975. At the very beginning the band consisted of Ron Cabel, lead guitar; Terry Hale, bass; Tommy Foote, drums; and Mike Daily, steel guitar. These four men had been playing on campus as a band with another singer, but they had just been fired from that gig by the singer. George read their advertisement on a campus bulletin board and gave them a call. The band had been performing under the name of Stoney Ridge. Mike's grandfather was Pappy Daily, the longtime manager of George Jones. They all seemed to hit it off perfectly, and George was on the path to a career in music.

"Didn't take but one line to know that he was the best singer I'd ever heard at that point in my life," Mike Daily claims. "We had our progressive [country] stuff that we had been used to playin', and kind of threw some of that in a little bit. I don't think George was ever real comfortable with any of that stuff."[11]

Performing at first as Ace in the Hole, the group's first booking was at a club called the Cheatham Street Warehouse, in San Marcos, Texas. This truly marked the professional singing debut of George Strait.

From the very start, George didn't fancy himself as a songwriter. He chose instead to interpret the songs of his country music idols. "I've always done other people's material. In the old days, that's all I did. I guess that's how I developed my style—by doing other people's material. When you are out there doing a four-hour club date and you're singing George Jones and Merle Haggard, that's what people want you to sound like. I don't do that anymore, but I think that helped."[12]

Texas is filled with all kinds of bars that feature music at night and almost every little town has a dance hall. It was in the Austin/San Antonio area where George Strait first became a sensation. There were a lot of places they could play, and they played most of the ones in the south and central Texas area. For a local band, they drew great crowds, becoming one of the top-drawing local bands around. Unlike most of the Top 40 bands playing the clubs back then, they didn't include any rock in their show. They only played country music—a lot of Bob Wills, a lot of Merle Haggard, and a lot of George Jones.

At this stage of the game, George and Ace in the Hole

were nothing more than a college town bar band. Their refusal to play popular rock & roll songs in their set was George's decision. "There were some clubs we never did play because of that," George recalls. "We wouldn't play Top 40, and we didn't break into a rock & roll song now and then, like a lot of bands thought they had to do. We just never did do it; we weren't going to do it. Still don't. It's not what we're going to do."[13]

Instead, George worked at perfecting his own style as a song interpreter. "When you're just a local act, and you're doing Merle Haggard and George Jones songs, people want you to sound like the records," he says. "So that's what you do; you sing like Merle or George. And pretty soon, that's just the way you sing. That's your style."[14]

There was a nice little circuit of nightclubs in the area for George and his band to appear at. Among the honky-tonks that they frequented were Gruene Hall in New Braunfels and The Broken Spoke in Austin. At the time, the drummer was Tom Foote. He is still with George, but now he is the road manager. Speaking about their band in the late '70s, Foote claims, "Even then George had a lot of musical integrity. We lost a few jobs because we wouldn't play Top 40 covers. But we were a great Texas dance band. He had the voice, he had the looks, and he was always focused. 1 saw the band as a way to keep from getting a job and a way to meet girls. George saw it as the future. We knew that if the train were going to pull out of the station, he would be the engineer."[15]

George has fond memories of those days. "You remember little things like back when you were carrying equipment around the back of a pickup, and traveling around four in a cab. You're trying to go do a show like ninety or a hundred, two hundred miles away. And packin' back up, carrying equipment out, loading it up and going back home the same night," he says.[16]

When you are young and just starting out in the business,

you tend to make mistakes that you hopefully learn from. George still remembers one night back in Texas on the bar circuit, where he made a definite faux pas. "Back then, we could do two or three hours of solid swing," he says. "That was our thing. That's what we liked to play. We opened up for the Playboys one time, and here we were doing their music, opening up their show for them. We were too stupid to realize what we were doing. We were doing exactly the same songs they were planning on doing. They're standing on the side of the stage watching us. We were kind of excited about that, but they were probably standing there thinking, 'Those boys are playing our swing! What in the world do they think they're doing?' I mean *they* were the guys. I will never forget that. It was really clueless on our part. We were really doing it because we love it so much. It wasn't that we were trying to steal their music or be better than them or even compete with them. We were real clueless about what we were doing, but we were doing it out of respect and honor. I don't think they quite took it that way."[17]

According to George, he had found his niche doing songs like "Take Me Back to Tulsa" and "Milk Cow Blues." Bob Wills & His Playboys' music was extremely popular in the Texas dance halls, and that was the kind of music George and his band stuck with. They played "Fraulein" and "Whiskey River" from Johnny Cash, and tunes made popular by Ray Price, George Jones, Merle Haggard, Bob Wills, Hank Thompson, and Webb Pierce. They were playing the type of music they liked, and developing a great following doing it.

Comparing it to the way things are nowadays for him, George says, "Now we have sound people and light people, and I go and do a sound check and everything's already there. Where back when we were hooking it all up ourselves, and loading it and unloading it and so, you tend to forget about that."[18]

Country music in those days seemed to belong to men in sequined suits and women in big hair. Johnny Cash, Hank Williams, Jr., Lynn Anderson, Freddie Fender, and Johnny Paycheck were among the top acts. There was also a local Texas music scene that was happening. George and the band were very aware of who was catching on, performers like Jerry Jeff Walker and Michael Martin Murphey.

In was Mike Daily's dad, Don Daily, who was the first to really recognize the commercial potential in George's singing. "I encouraged them to come in and make a record," says Don, who brought them to Houston to record for the family-owned label, D Records. It was the same label that first recorded Willie Nelson when he was just an aspiring songwriter. "And they thought, well, they could use it to book some dances, using it for a promo copy. And of course once we put it out, already being in the distributing business, and having a promotion man and so forth, we thought we'd go ahead and try to sell it. Which didn't have any success. We had a few small radio stations play it. That was about it."[19]

While all of this was happening, a very important person had come into George's life. His name was Erv Woolsey. From 1969 to 1975, Erv had worked for several record companies around the country, including Warner Brothers, ABC, and 20th Century. In 1975 he returned to his hometown of San Marcos and opened his own nightclub, The Prairie Rose. George and Ace in the Hole performed at The Prairie Rose.

Erv Woolsey recalls, "The first time I heard George sing, I was standing in the back of the club with my back to him. When I heard him crank up, I just had to turn around and see who was singing. I knew right then he was a great singer. So I introduced myself and started talking to him. I know at first he was a little skeptical of me, but we went on to become great friends."[20]

After a year in the nightclub business, Erv tired of it and sold it. He moved back to Nashville, where he landed a job as the promotions head for MCA Records. Fortunately, George held on to Erv's phone number when he headed back into the music industry, first in Chicago, and when here located in Nashville. Knowing Erv was later to prove a handy contact.

With Mike's dad, Don Daily, producing from 1976 to 1979, George and Ace in the Hole recorded eight songs. It was during these years that Strait first put pen to paper in an attempt at becoming a songwriter himself. Among these songs were "I Just Can't Go on Dying Like This," "(That Don't Change) The Way I Feel about You," and "I Don't Want to Talk It Over Anymore."

"I had written three songs that we did," he explains. "On the 'B' side of each one was a song by someone else, one by Clay Blaker, maybe two. Anyway, I wrote these songs, and you might be able to hear, when you listen to these songs, why my song-writing didn't develop the way I wanted it to. They're not bad songs, but you can see what a rookie I was, just a young guy trying to get started in country music."[21]

Listening to these three songs, it is easy to hear that George's voice is expressive and full sounding. However, the cuts are not very commercial. "I Just Can't Go on Dying Like This" is a clever turn of phrase on a medium-tempo number that properly conjures up images of crying in one's beer at a honky-tonk. George sounds a bit stiff on this cut, like he can't quite get comfortable in front of the microphone. "(That Don't Change) The Way I Feel about You" is a pleasant ballad that tries a little too hard to be "country." It is dull and twangy. Still not quite it. "I Don't Want to Talk It Over Anymore" is the best of the trio. Much more care is given to the way George is miked. There is a deep, resonant quality to his voice that sounds excellent. However, there are very distracting female background vocals that are ill-suited to the song and are too loud in the mix.

Among the songs that he penned back then were rudimentary versions of his later hits "Lonesome Rodeo Cowboy" and "Right or Wrong."

He was very fussy about his songs, even at the beginning. He focused on the melody first thing, and if he liked it enough, he'd begin paying closer attention to the lyrics. If both measured up, he'd decide to do it.

At the time, George and his band were quite proud of the songs that they had recorded, despite none of them setting the world on fire or attracting the attention of a major record label.

In an attempt to jump start their musical careers in 1977, George, songwriter Darryl Staedtler, and Kent Finlay—who owned the Cheatham Street Warehouse—all drove up to Nashville from Texas. Staedtler had a music publishing deal with Chappel Music, and he wrangled George a shot at recording the songwriter's demos in Music City, which he could in turn use as singing demos. That day in the recording studio, George laid down six of Darryl's songs, including "80 Proof Bottle of Tear Stopper," which he would later include on his 1983 *Right or Wrong* album.

They stayed at the Hall of Fame Motor Inn, and George went down to the bar and sang with the band. However, things just didn't seem to click in Nashville. Although he really wanted a record deal, it didn't materialize. They shopped the demos around, pitching them to a few labels. George returned to Texas without a deal.

Although it didn't look like they were making any career progress, George was gaining some life-long friends, and gaining the respect of several of his peers. Among them, Ray Benson of the modern-day Texas swing band Asleep at the Wheel. Ray remembers very distinctly the first time he heard George Strait's singing. "It was 1978," says Benson. "We were playing at Gruene Hall near New Braunfels,

Texas, a hundred-year-old dance hall in an old south Texas German town. I was sitting on the bus listening to the opening band who was doing all the Texas dance hall standards, and to my delight some old Western swing numbers. The lead singer had a great voice; but I couldn't see him, and when I asked who the band was, they said, 'Ace in the Hole.' Well, we played the show, and I didn't think about the opening act much until a number of months later when this record came out called 'Unwound.' The guy's name was George Strait, and my friend said, 'He's that guy in the Ace in the Hole band.' "[22]

George was beginning to become exhausted by his routine. In 1978 he was in his senior year in college, worked on the ranch that his dad had inherited from his grandparents, and at night he was a singer with the band. Several more road trips to Nashville yielded little more than shattered dreams of stardom: "Drove all night, stayed at the Hall of Fame Motor Inn, did a session with some musician friends of mine, and pitched it around town with no luck at all. [By 1979]I was just fixin' to go ahead and quit. I was twenty-seven years old, I'd been playing for six or seven years, and I was beginning to think I just wasn't good enough and maybe ought to try something else. I gave my band notice and signed up for a full-time job with this outfit in Uvalde, Texas, that designed cattle pens. But a week before I was to report for the job, I realized I just couldn't do it. And I decided to give it one more year."[23]

George figured that it was now or never. "I knew I didn't want to be fifty years old and playing in bars and honky-tonks. I felt what I wanted to do was be with a major label, making records and doing what I'm doing now. I didn't feel like I was making any progress . . . I thought maybe it was just something I dreamed up and it's never going to happen," he recalls.[24]

Norma Strait recalls her husband's mental state around this time of indecision very specifically. According to her,

"George was moping around the house so much I couldn't stand it. I figured I didn't want to live in Uvalde with him like that, so we talked about his hopes in music. I wanted him to give it one more try."[25]

Although George's dad would seem to be among those most critical of his plans, he didn't try to talk him out of his musical aspirations. "My father, I think, after I started playing, encouraged me somewhat with music. But I can't blame him if he looked at it from a practical angle. I mean, he knew how many tried, but how few succeeded.

"I'd think about that all the time," he exclaims, "all the time! Especially after I'd been at it awhile and nothing much was happening. Of course, all my friends would tell me, 'You sound great!' but I couldn't help thinking they were just saying that because they *were* my friends. It especially got to me after I'd made a couple of trips to Nashville and did some sessions that I thought were really good, and the labels all turned them down."[26]

It seemed like everyone had their own opinion about what he was doing wrong, or what he could do to become more successful at what he was doing. His cowboy hat seemed to come up in conversations time and time again. "I had quite a few people tell me, 'Take the hat off,' but I never would." He laughs. "It's just that I identify with that sort of cowboy; those are the sort of people I run around with. I don't know, it's just a way of life."[27]

Erv Woolsey recalls the singer's strong convictions even back in the early days. "George came along when country music was not exactly the darling of Nashville. I'm from Texas, too, so I can identify with George. I remember people wantin' him to wear those shirts with the studs on them, and bell bottom jeans, because they thought that was just the cool thing to do. But George fought all that from day one," he says.[28]

In 1980 George confessed his dilemma to Erv Woolsey. Erv listened to all of Strait's music, and he came up with a plan. Woolsey invited him to come up to Nashville to record three songs that he could in turn shop around to some of the major record labels in town. Record producer Blake Mevis was a friend of Woolsey's, and Erv thought that Blake was cutting some great songs for acts like The Kendalls, and Vern Gosdin. He also felt that Mevis would be able to spend some time with Strait and really deliver some impressive recordings.

Blake Mevis was later to recall that he was less than knocked over when he first heard George sing. Erv Woolsey had brought Blake down to the small college town where George had an established following, so that the producer could see him confidently in his element. Says Mevis, "It was back in the fall of 1980 in a small honky-tonk in San Marcos, Texas, that I first met George Strait. He was fronting a small Texas swing band singing songs that everyone in the joint knew and danced to and that I had never heard before. I must confess that it wasn't apparent to me at first glance, the monumental potential that George possessed, but at the urging of my good friend, Erv Woolsey, we decided to cut a few sides on George in the studio, and shop for a [major recording] deal."[29]

The three songs that they recorded were "Nobody in His Right Mind Would've Left Her," "The Perfect Lie," and Darryl Staedtler's "Blame it on Mexico." With George's singing talent, and Erv's confidence in him, they began shopping for a recording deal. With the ranching job in Uvalde still hovering in the distance as a career move, it was "now or never" as far as Strait's musical career was concerned.

Chapter Three

"Up Close and Personal"

George Strait's sense of privacy is unlike anyone else's in popular music today. While country performers regularly appear on the cover of *People* magazine, the *Star*, or the *National Enquirer*, George has held his ground, and refused to publicly speak about his private life. With the exception of speaking briefly about his wife, Norma, and his son, Bubba, and admitting that he lives in the center of Texas, he prefers to chat briefly about his career and his music, and then cuts the conversation off when it veers too close to his well-protected homelife. Even his band members are very closemouthed about Strait, out of respect for his wishes.

Tracking down people to speak candidly about George is like looking for needles in a haystack. However, if you are on the Internet, and you do a "George Strait" search, you will find that there are several Web Pages. Among them are a brief MCA Records press biography and two very notable pages created by some of George's biggest admirers. One of them is "The George Strait Home Page," and it is maintained by a very friendly and informative fan of George's named Troy Sniff. The other one is "So You Like George Strait?" and is about the early years of the quiet Mr. Strait. What makes the "So You Like George Strait?" page so fascinating is that it was written by someone who has known him since the mid-1970s. At the time, George Strait was just a local Texas hopeful singer, fronting a bar band. He had just teamed up with the Ace in the Hole band, which included Mike Daily. In those early days, George and the band were often playing to nearly empty little clubs in the San Marcos area, and extra audience members were heartily welcomed, even if they were just enough bodies to fill up an empty seat or two.

At the time, Mike Daily's younger brother, David, was a high school student who was more into rock & roll than he was country. However, the prospect of tagging along with his older brother and hanging out in nightclubs or backstage at concerts was fun. Now, over twenty years later, it is David Daily who created and maintains the "So You Like George Strait?" Web Page.

I was fortunate enough to track down David Daily at his home in Texas. Not only did I find him to be friendly and enthusiastic, but he was most informative on the subject of young George Strait. What was it like to have seen George and his band progress from playing in small bars and clubs near San Marcos, and to watch him become a country music superstar? David Daily knows, because he was there from the very beginning, watching from the sidelines.

Although David now has a regular job working for the local government in his native Texas, he takes great interest in maintaining his Web Page on Strait, and in hearing from friends and fans through it. The following conversation took place August 11, 1996:

BEGO: I find George Strait to be a very likable character. However, it has been very difficult to find people close to him who are willing to talk about him. Because he is so private about his private life.

DAILY: I imagine that is kind of a difficult task, as compared with a lot of people.

BEGO: As I understand it, you met George in the very beginning of his career.

DAILY: Yes, I have an old video tape of George, and I have one with audio tape on it. My dad used to film him with one of the original VCR cameras . . .

BEGO: That sounds like the kind of footage a television producer like Dick Clark would like to get his hands on.

DAILY: I have video from one of the early, early shows.

BEGO: So, you've known George for quite a while, haven't you?

DAILY: Well, my brother [Mike] has been playing with him since . . . [1975]. . . . It was so long ago that I can't remember the exact date of the first time I saw George, or met George, it's been so long. . . . My brother had a band called Stoney Ridge, and they had a Spanish singer who sang with them, and he had some contacts with Waylon Jennings, or something like that, and they were going to try and do some recording with RCA [Records], but I don't think it ever panned out. 'Cause he left the band, and they [Stoney Ridge] put that ad for a singer to front the band.

BEGO: Now, this would have been in San Marcos?

DAILY: Right. I think they were just putting up ads on the bulletin boards at the university as a matter of fact. And they were doing some auditions for singers. I don't actually know if they auditioned anybody but George—he must have been the first and last one! (laughs)

BEGO: Well, they definitely picked a good one. Do you recall seeing him the first time performing?

DAILY: I was trying to think of that one today, and that's a tough one to do. One tape that I do have was a Memorial Park political benefit for Representative Bob Kruger, and this was down here in Houston. He was running for a Senate seat or something, and they had a beer/barbecue thing out here in Memorial Park, and that's where I have the tape from, that my dad had taken. . . . He would take us along to see him play. I don't know exactly the first time I saw George. . . . It would have been late 1974, or early 1975. Somewhere in that area. Like I say, it's hard to pinpoint it. It was a long time ago. I can't believe my brother has even been playing that long! It's crazy.

BEGO: . . . Those first times, or the first couple of times you saw him performing, I assume you came to see your brother Mike playing, because George was just an unknown singer at that time.

DAILY: Yeah. I didn't know George, and he didn't mean anything to me particularly at the time.

BEGO: Taking that into consideration, what did you think of George personally, both as a performer and as a person—both onstage and offstage?

DAILY: Well, the first few times I saw him, I thought he was really good. Of course, my dad being in the music business for, gosh, I don't know how many years at that point—thirty or thirty-five—he was real excited about George. I was pretty much into rock & roll at the time. I didn't listen to country music. But, to have my brother playing in a band in front of a bunch of people, that was great. Whereas, George's singing—I thought that was great. I thought they were good, considering that they hadn't been playing together that long. It was new to me. I didn't know what to compare him with. I'd listened to some country music over the years, but not a lot. . . . In the early days, usually, backstage, I wouldn't ever really talk to George very much. He was either with his wife or had family all around. He was very quiet and very shy. . . . I mean, we'd say "Hi," or this or that, but he didn't do a lot of talking back then. And, I wasn't into country music that much back then.

BEGO: So, you didn't have a lot of burning questions to ask him.

DAILY: . . . He was a cowboy from the country, and I was a rock & roller from the city; so there wasn't a lot there [for me] in the early days.

BEGO: But, you remember him as being very nice? He seems like a down-to-earth nice guy.

DAILY: He was always real nice. He'd always talk to you and say "Hi," things like that. If we had any conversation back then, he and I, it really wasn't anything that sticks out at that time. . . . He was thinner back then. He was a pretty lean-looking guy. Of course, he's not big now or nothing; but he was really thin back then, and his hair was long—not real long, but it came down over the back of his neck. He used to wear a baseball cap, and in one of the video tapes I have, he had the baseball cap on. That's pretty unusual. You don't usually see him onstage with a baseball cap.

BEGO: . . . Those would be rare photos.

DAILY: That would have been before the cowboy hats came in.

BEGO: I'd love to get a photo.

DAILY: The only problem is the quality of the video, but my brother, he's sitting down. They're playing in a little covered stage, and the angle of the sun—my brother's in [focus] good, but the [other] members of the band are a little darker, because of the angle of the sun. You can see good enough to see who it is, but . . . I don't know how good it would look if it was transferred to [still] pictures. . . .

BEGO: Back then, what was the musical set like? They were playing a lot of Texas swing, weren't they? A lot of Bob Wills & His Texas Playboys?

DAILY: Yeah. Today they've got so much hit material, they can't play as much of it like they did. A couple of the old ones like "Milk Cow Blues," and stuff like that. They did a lot of Ray Price, Bob Wills, Merle Haggard, a few George Jones songs. Of course they always have their popular ones like "Amarillo by Morning," they have played in their set for the longest time. And "South of the Border." . . . They did a song that was always really popular; it was called "The Last Kiss."

BEGO: The one about the car accident?

DAILY: Yeah, that's the one. He used to do that, and the crowd always used to request that one: "Play that, play that!"

BEGO: . . . That's got to be about as close to rock & roll as George Strait has ever been.

DAILY: Yeah, it really wasn't a country song. I remember it from when I was a kid. It must have come out in the early '60s, or mid '60s. . . . I have the single somewhere at home.

BEGO: I can hear the song: "Oh, where oh where can my baby be?"

DAILY: Exactly. And they used to play that all the time. I've got to find out who recorded that song.

BEGO: I think it was originally done by J. Frank Wilson.

DAILY: You're right. And you see, my dad was a record distributor, so I have all kinds of contacts to find old records like that. They played that quite a bit, and that was always real popular.

BEGO: Have you been to any of George's Team Roping Classic events there in Texas?

DAILY: No, the only rodeo event I have been to is the rodeo down here in Houston [in the 1980s]. . . . I remember my brother calling down and saying that they got a call that Eddie Rabbitt was sick, or—I heard another story to the contrary. (laughs) . . . He couldn't make the show, and it wasn't many hours later when I found out—I think it was about noon or one o'clock that day that they were gonna be playing at the rodeo. I thought, "Man, I don't believe this!" I don't know who called.

BEGO: Was this before they were signed to the record deal?

DAILY: No, I believe they had already released "Unwound" and the first album [*Strait Country*]. That had just come out, and they had the original material to play. I don't think the second album was out. They might have been working on it. They wouldn't have gotten called in if they didn't have any original music. At the time, "Unwound" was taking off. I remember, "Fool Hearted Memory" was on that album. I have a picture of George taken backstage at The Crystal Chandelier in Brownsville, Texas, when the first Number One record went Number One. I don't know if that was before or after the rodeo performance, but they used to play at that club a lot. That was during [the run of] the first album, so they were still playing a lot in clubs.

BEGO: What was the mid-Texas music scene like back then? Was it just a bunch of college bars?

DAILY: Yeah. In San Marcos you had the bar scene, which changed a lot. One month or two months there'd be a club here or there, and then it may close down. It would depend . . . they would move around quite a bit. Of course around 1980, when disco became quite big, they began changing around some of the clubs. It was mostly college kids at a lot of the clubs. When they first started playing, there were three clubs right off of the feeder off of [Highway] 35. One of them I think was called The Getaway, the other one was Rose Hall, and the other one was The Cheyenne Social Club. . . . I guess it would be on the east side of San Marcos. They used to play there all of the time.

I remember going in, and there may be ten or fifteen people in the whole club. I might have seen George for the first time in one of those three clubs, as opposed to Memorial Park, but I don't exactly remember which one it was. But it was amazing. They'd be up there playing, and there'd be ten or fifteen people in there; and a couple of them would be me and my friends. You could dance all you wanted to, or whatever you wanted to do. Looking back on it, it is strange, but of course back then it wasn't. And that would be on slow nights, and of course there would be a lot of people. It just depended on the clubs they played. I know that there was a club called Cheatham Street Warehouse that was real popular. Alvin Crow used to play there all the time; I think Willie Nelson played there, too, several times. It was a real popular place. A lot of people used to go there. I don't even know if that place is still open or not. It was like a tin barn on top of a structure, almost like a feed house. . . . It was built two or three feet off of the ground, and the floor was wood: plywood sheets nailed down to the floor. It was different, that's for sure! Very different.

BEGO: So, it was like a big ol' barn dance?

DAILY: Yes, except that it wasn't that big. But they had a bar there, and a stage. It was one of the places to be in San Marcos in those days, though. As far as clubs being real popular—that was the one.

BEGO: You mean The Crystal Chandelier?

DAILY: Cheatham Street Warehouse.

BEGO: . . . Were you impressed with the music at that time? I know that you were more into rock & roll.

DAILY: Yes, I was impressed, but it was more exciting or interesting to me because my brother played in the band. He was playing at all of the hot clubs, and I would get to go in for free, more than being all excited about the music. I didn't even know how to dance, or anything back then. . . . It was a couple of years before I graduated [high school]. Of course, back at that time I wasn't really old enough to go to clubs, but back then you could still get in easily.

BEGO: [Is] that when your dad signed George and the Ace in the Hole band to their first recording contract?

DAILY: Right.

BEGO: Then didn't he take George and the band into the studio to record those first demos? You mention on your George Strait computer home page that they went into Doggett's Recording Studio, on Studemont Street in Houston. . . . Were you there for those sessions at all?

DAILY: The first one, where they recorded "I Can't Go on Dying Like This" and "The Honky Tonk Downstairs." I was there for that. . . . [It] was about two blocks down from my dad's record distributorship, down the street . . . and a lot of local people recorded there. . . . It was a place where a lot of musicians who were trying to break out [in show business] would go in. . . . It was cheap, [and] you wouldn't have to pay a fortune.

BEGO: So, you were there for that first recording session. What was it like? I assume that because your dad was in the business, you had been to recording sessions before?

DAILY: No, actually I never had been.

BEGO: So this was the first recording session you had ever been to?

DAILY: Right, so that made it real exciting for me, too. The studio was kind of like a ... well, I don't know if you've ever been to Houston or not. It is in the old part of town where my dad's business was, called The Heights. It's a lot of one-story, or two-story wooden houses. It's kind of hard to explain, but that was what the studio looked like. It was probably made out of a house that they had bought.

BEGO: Is that that area that sort of surrounds a square downtown?

DAILY: No, actually it's north of I-10, north of downtown. It actually used to be considered downtown Houston, before there was the modern downtown Houston. Like I said, it had some wooden houses and some brick structures around there, and it looked like the studio was built out of a house; and I never went to the upstairs part—the second level. But, the downstairs, you would walk in, and they had the little glass booths there, and you walked off to the left, and that's where the band set up and everything, and played. It was all new to me. . . . I don't know what type of machine the guy was using to record, because I didn't know that much about it. I don't know what kind of equipment he had or, I can't even remember what his name was; but my dad knew him pretty good, so they set up the session.

BEGO: And, you sat in the control booth?

DAILY: Yes, and watched my dad sit there and produce. They would do several takes over and over. It took a little while, but in a couple of days, I think they had both of the songs done. The quality of the studio was pretty good back then, and the songs came out good, I thought. You know, we used to listen to those records all the time—over and over. And, everybody who I meet today is interested in them. I guess that MCA and George were selling those records years back, at some of the shows and stuff. . . . But, before then, people used to really go crazy whenever I would play one of those records for them. They would say, "Golly!" They were really amazed to listen to a George Strait record they hadn't heard.

BEGO: Now that original version of "I Can't Go on Dying Like This" is on George's *Strait Out of the Box* boxed set. So, you were quite impressed with what you saw and heard in the studio that day?

DAILY: Yeah, it was really great. I had never seen anybody play a fiddle or violin, and then George singing. He had to sit there and do it, of course, over and over, and change it a little bit here and a little bit there to go along with the music, so that was real interesting. Of course, it all sounded pretty good to me, and my dad would make some changes on stuff, and redo the end, so it sounded a lot better. Of course, it was new to them [George and Ace in the Hole] because they hadn't done it either.

BEGO: Did you ever dream at the time that they would have such a big career as they've ended up having, and that George has had?

DAILY: Well, not at that time probably, but after the second record, I guess, and all of the clubs they were playing, and things, it was like: man—this guy's great! His voice is great—it's incredible. At that point I started listening to other country music, more Merle Haggard, George Jones, . . . and Moe Bandy—I used to listen to him quite a bit.

And then I started realizing how good [George] is. And then, of course, my dad being the music distributor—or what is called an independent distributor. Back then, all of the major record companies went through local independent record distributors instead of doing it on their own. We represented ABC Records, London Records, Motown Records, and a couple of others. We had five or six big labels that we did, so we had a PR [public relations] man who did all of the radio stations in town. . . . In other words—whenever new records would come out from Motown or London Records, or A&M or whoever, he would send the records off to the radio station for them to play, listen to, or do whatever they wanted to do. So we had him on staff to try and push George's [D Records] releases. However, at the radio stations, when they opened up the promotional package, and they didn't see Warner Brothers Records, or Motown . . .

BEGO: Or one of the big labels . . .

DAILY: Yeah, so it was kind of a drag. They were like: "Oh, we aren't gonna play this; it's not gonna be anything noteworthy."

BEGO: So no one wanted to play the records at that point because it wasn't on a major label?

DAILY: Yeah. Of course, we only had a couple of stations. We had KIKK, and I guess KILT-AM was doing country back then. "Kick" [KIKK] had been around forever even back then, and there might have been a couple of local AM stations that were still doing music back then, but I don't remember. We sent the records off to all of them, and I think that my dad had talked to the music director at KIKK several times back then; but he just couldn't get them to play that first George Strait single on D Records. . . . Years later, after George's second album came out, and they were playing at Gilley's in Pasadena, Texas, and George's tour bus was parked out back, it was real funny. I went out back to the bus, and there was a whole bunch of people waiting in line to get back there to meet George; and I walked past everybody, because my brother would let me on the bus. And, the first guy in line was Joe Ladd, waiting there, trying to get on the bus, and saying to me, "Can I get on the bus?" I thought that was so funny. . . . About three years before that he wouldn't even play George's records on the radio! . . . I know that was his job, and that he just couldn't go and play anything that he wanted, but I was like: "Well, that serves you right!"

BEGO: . . . Basically, you were there from the very beginning to watch it all happen. If you were to describe George's personality—from your perspective—how would you describe him?

DAILY: I would say he's a shy guy. He's a lot like me. That's the way I am basically, a reserved type of person. I'm quiet, and not too outgoing unless someone approaches me. I don't think he's the type of person who approaches people. I think he's a family-oriented type person. I think he pretty much believes in that: the family. He's got a good personality—if you get in a situation where he is comfortable, and you can see his personality. I guess if he's not around people that he knows real well, then he's not going to be real open; so you have to be in a comfortable situation, and he'll laugh and joke. He will open up a little bit. He's changed a lot in the past ten or fifteen years, from the early days. I think that it's getting used to interviews and stuff like that. . . . I think he's a lot more comfortable. I've seen him on some of the country shows that are on cable, doing interviews, and he seems pretty relaxed, comfortable, and his good humor seems to be real good. He's not as nervous as he used to be in the earlier days. It probably just took him a while to learn how to handle the tension, I'm sure, like anybody. He's always nice and cordial. I never saw him get upset. I saw him a lot of times. Of course, I wasn't around him every minute all the time, but. . . . Usually, if you are around people very much, you'll maybe see them lose their temper at least once. You know, upset them, to the point where they go off a little bit. But I never saw anything like that out of George.

BEGO: . . . He seems very even keeled. . . . You're not in regular contact with him at the moment, are you?

DAILY: The last time I saw him was probably at the Summit about three years ago, and I just saw him briefly, in passing. They were walking through the hall. George said, "How you doing?" and shook my hand, and then they rushed him off—all of the people around him. Then before that, it was probably seven or eight years ago at the Astrodome in his dressing room. I was going to go in and say "Hi," but his family was there. That's the way it got over the years. It got to a point where he had so many people after him, and so many people wanting to see him, that I just wasn't going to force my way in to talk to him anymore. Working for my dad, I got concert tickets and backstage passes to all of the great rock stars who came to town, and I went through all of that backstage thing for all those years. I doubt that he even talks very much to my brother. Because they go on and play, and they're gone. They're on separate busses. There came a point where I said, "I'm not gonna mess with it." A lot of people I'd take to shows, and they'd say, "Let's go backstage and say 'hello' to George," and I'd have to say, "No, I don't do that." I spent too many years getting autographs for girlfriends and stuff. I quit that a long time ago.

BEGO: It's fascinating that you have the perspective of having seen him so long ago, and are able to compare it to the phenomenon he is in the 1990s, to have watched it all happen.

DAILY: It was real exciting for me, especially when they appeared at the rodeo here in Houston; that's when it all took off. That catapulted them quickly into popularity. Of course, they would have made it anyway, or at least he would have made it. It might have taken a little bit longer, but that helped it along—a whole lot.

BEGO: What inspired you to put together this Web Page?

DAILY: My wife and one of her girlfriends said to me, "Hey, you ought to put something on the Internet. You're doing all of these popular pages. Why not put something about George on there?" I finally decided, "What the heck," and started messing with it. I put up a little bit of information, and people started checking it out, and they started sending me E-mail, and I thought, "This is incredible." The next thing I know Troy Sniff got in touch with me. He wanted to get sanctioned to do the official Web Page. I didn't have any problem with that, because I wasn't interested in it. All that I could really do was to ask my brother, and he'd have to ask George, and there were just too many channels to go through.

BEGO: By the time you went through all of that. . . .

DAILY: Yeah, there was not a lot I could have done for him. Every time I could mention a good word about Troy, I did, because I liked his page. I was impressed with everything that he has done, because he looks like he is totally dedicated. But, I do a lot of Web Pages and marketing, and selling advertisements. Eventually it became a way to create traffic for other pages.

BEGO: Is that what you do for a living now?

DAILY: No . . . I work full-time during the day, and I just do that in my spare time and in the evenings. . . . I work for Harris County in the purchasing department. . . . and then I come home and I work on the Web Pages. It seems like that's what I spend most of my time doing—trying to make money at it.

BEGO: What is the Web address of your page?

DAILY: It's http://www.concom.com/patriot/george.htm

Chapter Four

"Strait to the Top"

It was 1980, and George Strait was stuck on the middle of the fence. Was he going to rope cattle for a living or was he going to lasso a recording deal in Nashville? Some of the variables he could control, but others were totally out of his hands. Was he going to make his mark in the music world or was he going to spend the rest of his days branding cows and horses?

The country music scene from 1979 to 1981 was a changing one. The boundary lines between country music and pop music were getting fuzzier during these years. Several country singers were ending up on the pop charts, and many of the pop and rock music performers were ending up on the country charts. Hollywood was getting into the scene as well, with country-themed movies and their successful soundtrack albums.

Many of the men and women who were driving forces in country music at the time were losing a degree of their clout. Johnny Cash, Lynn Anderson, Loretta Lynn, Waylon Jennings, and Conway Twitty were all beginning to feel the crunch in strong hits. Only Willie Nelson seemed immune to the changing tastes in country music, and part of the reason was that he had always been as much a pop singer as he was a country star.

The old guard of Nashville was being replaced on the charts by more crossover country/pop/folk/rock artists like The Charlie Daniels Band, The Bellamy Brothers, Crystal Gayle, and Eddie Rabbitt. Bridging the gap between the two generations of performers were Mickey Gilley, Ronnie Milsap, and Dolly Parton—each of whom found their greatest degree of chart success from 1975 to 1985.

Two very important movies were released in 1980 that dealt with middle-American country life and exciting, bigger-than-life characters. More importantly, they spawned two very successful soundtrack albums, and suddenly the spotlight was on Nashville. The first of these two films was *Coal Miner's Daughter,* which was based on the autobiography of Loretta Lynn. In addition to having Sissy Spacek portraying Lynn to perfection, Beverly D'Angelo as Patsy Cline made the movie a top box-office hit. The soundtrack album became a Gold Top 20 hit, and there was a sudden increase in sales of Patsy Cline's original recordings.

The following month, the John Travolta/Debra Winger movie *Urban Cowboy* became a huge hit. Not only did it suddenly become chic to ride mechanical bulls, and party all night at Mickey Gilley's real Texas nightclub (in Pasadena, outside of Houston), but the sales of cowboy boots and hats went up as well.

All of a sudden, country music experienced an upsurgence in sales. The soundtrack album went on to become one of the biggest-selling albums in country music history. It was certified Platinum for having sold a million copies and peaked at Number Three on the American pop charts. The album featured several established country acts like Kenny Rogers, Mickey Gilley, Johnny Lee, and The

Charlie Daniels Band. In addition, it featured several pop music artists doing countrified material. Several established rockers like Dan Fogelberg, Linda Ronstadt & John David Souther, Jimmy Buffett, Joe Walsh, and Bonnie Raitt all contributed their own country tunes to the album. Because of this, suddenly a fresh batch of young rock & roll loving kids were exposed to country music in a context they could relate to. Just to give the proceedings some rock & roll power, the soundtrack also included previously released cuts by The Eagles, Bob Seger & The Silver Bullet Band, and Boz Scaggs.

It was also that same year that something unique happened on the country music charts. The group Alabama released its first in a solid string of million-selling albums, and became the first group to capture fans of both rock & roll and country music. With younger audiences responding to these new acts, record companies were suddenly looking for fresh talent to revitalize the whole country music scene. This was to be George Strait's big window of opportunity.

At this point, George knew what he wanted. He recalls, "Finally, my big goal became getting a record company to sign me to a contract. That's every singer's dream out there. It took a while, I gotta admit. It took about seven or eight years of consistently playing the honky-tonks before I was ever signed with MCA Records, and don't think that was because I wasn't trying! I had been in Nashville two or even three times trying to cut sessions that would work. My demos were pitched around town with no luck whatsoever!"[30]

With Erv in his corner in Nashville, the big push was undeniably under way to sign George at MCA. Ron Chancey was vice president of A&R for MCA Records. Urged by Erv Woolsey, then head of promotion for the label, he went to Texas to see George and his band perform in a small Texas bar. Although he thought George sang and looked great, he was doing a lot of Western swing, and Chancey didn't think the music was very commercial.

Erv Woolsey brought then MCA Nashville chief Jim Fogelsong some of George Strait's demos to listen to. While he thought that George sang very well, he failed to hear anything special enough about the songs or the performances to offer him a contract.

Although MCA passed on George, Erv just wouldn't let up on his push to land him on the label. Says Chancey, "The first time I went down and saw him I didn't recommend that he get signed because he was doing just about all Western swing. He was doing too much of it. . . . About three or four months later, we went to see him again. He was doing some more commercial type stuff. I saw him, came back, went to talk to Jim and said he ought to give him a shot."[31]

Finally, in the beginning of 1981, MCA gave George Strait his lucky break. They offered him a single deal. This meant that the company would release a one-song single by George, and if it was successful on the radio, and in sales, then they would give him a shot at a whole album. George remembers that he had his fingers crossed that things would go his way, and that the single would grow into a whole LP.

George still feels the excitement of that day that he put his "John Hancock" on his first recording contract. "I remember when I first signed with MCA Records, and I went into their offices in Nashville. I remember lookin' at all those Gold records on the wall and thinking, 'Good grief, man!' I remember I even asked Erv, my manager, 'Hey, Erv, you think I'll ever have one of those?' So, it's really been like a dream come true," he laughs.[32]

The song "Unwound" came to be recorded by George Strait by a roundabout path. Originally it was Tom Collins, Blake Mevis' music publisher, who suggested it. It was written by aspiring songwriter/performer Dean Dillon and his writing partner, Frank Dycus. Collins told Woolsey he would finance a demo session for George if they'd use his song. Woolsey listened to Dean Dillon's demo of "Unwound" and knew it was the kind of song that could break George. Although it wasn't a great demo—Dean sounded like he had been up all night making the tape—Woolsey knew he had a hit.

Frank Dycus had been intending to pitch the song to Johnny Paycheck. Paycheck's "Take This Job and Shove It" became one of the biggest hits of the '70s when it was released in 1978. What could have been Paycheck's big follow-up single, instead became the catapult to launch George Strait's career.

February 2, 1981—Ground Hog Day. If a ground hog emerges from his home on that day, whether he sees his own shadow is supposed to predict the pattern of winter weather for the next six weeks. Like the ground hog, George Strait went into the studio that day to record the one song that was going to predict his future. Strait emerged from the studio with a song that everyone agreed had hit potential. It was called "Unwound."

It was a song that was immediately recognizable as destined for radio success. With the quick-paced tempo, infectious fiddle work, and imaginative lyrics, "Unwound" seemed to appeal to everyone. "I figured it would do well, and not just in Texas. As a promotion man, I knew that in those days the program directors at stations across Texas and the Southwest and Midwest were traditional country fans. And they would listen to and add a promising new artist to the playlist, especially if they were traditional," Erv recalls.[33]

"Traditional" started cropping up from the very start of George Strait's recording career. He didn't court the title in any way, but he was to be dubbed as the banner-waving leader of the "new traditionalist" wave in the 1980s in Nashville. For George, he was just being himself. However, it was to become the prevailing opinion of critics, press, and other artists.

"It's a label I got stuck with, and it doesn't bother me," George explains. "I love that kind of music. Whatever I do is certainly country. It might not all be as hard-core country as some of the songs I do. But I think maybe it's in the hat or the way I dress that also goes into it."[34]

Garth Brooks in the 1990s stated that George Strait was his number one idol. He claimed that hearing "Unwound" made the decision for him as to what he wanted to do.

George was flabbergasted that he had actually pulled it off, and had landed a major label deal. He later admitted there were so many big acts on the MCA Records label at the time—Loretta Lynn, Conway Twitty, The Oak Ridge Boys, Merle Haggard, Tanya Tucker—that he thought his record would get pushed under the pile.

The single was released in May, and the week of the 16th, "Unwound" entered the country charts in *Billboard* magazine, and proceeded to climb into the Top Ten. George will never forget the day that he first heard his voice on the radio. He was back in San Marcos, working on his day job on the ranch, when it came across the airwaves. "I was shocked. I couldn't believe it. I mean, hearing your first record on the radio, when it was something that you had been trying to get to for so long, and then finally having it happen, it was wild. Here I was driving around the ranch there, and I'd hear it go up the chart [week by week], and I'm saying to myself: 'What's wrong with this picture? I've got a hit record. I need to go out on the road and go play some concerts.' "[35]

George was very well aware that the sound of country radio had drastically changed since the previous year's *Urban Cowboy* mania had struck. Suddenly there was a swing away from producing songs in Nashville that had crossover potential to them. Bring back the fiddles and the pedal steel guitar, the new traditionalists were about to take over the town. People with radios were ready for some kind of change, and the record companies were responding to it. When George had first gone to Nashville, they'd said he was too country. Now, four years later, he was just country enough.

The tide had begun to turn for several people that year in country music. The year 1981 marked the big-time chart arrivals of Rosanne Cash, Earl Thomas Conlee, and the teaming of David Frizzell and Shelly West. John Anderson had a couple records just before George's. Ricky Skaggs, Reba McEntire, and the others were all doing basically the same kind of music, playing a more traditional sound than what had been played. They were going against the grain of the crossover music and reaching out to a traditional country music audience that was ready for more.

Several days later George was given the green light for his debut album. "Unwound" had become a huge Top Ten hit for him, eventually reaching Number Six on the country charts. George was well on his way now. He admits that he wasn't entirely convinced that it was actually as strong a song as it ended up being. However, he was thrilled by his newfound success on the charts with it.

During the first part of June, he was back in Nashville, this time accompanied by his Ace in the Hole band. The second week of the month he was featured at Nashville's big meet-the-stars annual fete: Fan Fair. Every night that week, George and the band performed at the Reflections Ballroom at the Radisson Hotel. During the day, George was in Music City Music Hall recording studios with producer Blake Mevis and a group of Nashville session musicians. This was to set a pattern for all of George's albums. Although he continued to play in concert with Ace in the Hole—with the exception of a special cut here and there— he exclusively utilized studio musicians when he was recording an album.

The album *Strait Country* was constructed out of the three

tracks he had recorded in February along with "Unwound," and seven additional cuts that were recorded that
June. George was not entirely pleased with every song that
finally made the album. But, as a rookie in town to play
in the big leagues, he decided that he had best just keep
his mouth shut and do what he was told to do, and record
what he was told to record.

Listening to the *Strait Country* album today, it is easy to
hear George as a diamond-in-the-rough, being polished
and set in his first year of recording. The song selections
reveal that clever turns of phrase were very big in country
music that year. Five out of ten songs on the album have
juxtaposing titles and/or lyrics, including "Down and
Out"; owning real estate or giving it away, "Every Time
You Throw Dirt on Her (You Lose a Little Ground)";
paradise or damnation, "She's Playing Hell Trying to Get
Me to Heaven"; strength and weakness, "Her Goodbye
Hit Me in the Heart"; and the concepts of being wound
and unwound on the initial hit "Unwound."

Also included on the album was Darryl Staedtler's ode
to romance and tequila south of the border, "Blame it on
Mexico." This song was one that George had recorded in
his first session with Blake Mevis in February, which had
also yielded "Perfect Lie" and "Nobody in His Right Mind
Would've Left Her." He ended up rerecording it to include
on *Strait Country*.

Other main highlights on the album were Blake Mevis
and David Wills' catchy and compelling "If You're Thinking You Want a Stranger (There's One Coming Home),"
and Dallas Frazier's drink-your-troubles-away tune about
one's wife being the waitress in the "Honky Tonk Downstairs." All in all, *Strait Country* was an offering of varied
country tunes which gave America its first look at country
music's great white-hatted hope: George Strait.

The photo on the cover of his first album, which was
taken by Tom Wilkes, depicts the singer in his well-worn,

cream-colored straw cowboy hat, an open shirt, and a sim-ple gold chain around his neck. He is standing against what looks like a tall fencepost, looking off to his right with a very plaintive look in his eye, like he is surveying the back forty acres of his ranch. It was about as unglitzy an image as one could have at the time. In a town peopled with rhinestone cowboys and Elvis wannabes, George represented the new wave in Nashville: real country, plain and simple.

The back of the original vinyl album cover showed a picture of Strait inside of Gruene Hall, back in Texas. This was the album that started it all, and Gruene Hall was one of the most memorable honky-tonks to have hosted his humble beginnings. It was fitting that it should be featured on *Strait Country*. (It was omitted from the currently available CD version of the album.)

When it came time to publicize his first album, George was to set several precedents that were to hold true for his entire career. Rule number one was to completely leave his family out of the limelight and out of his press interviews. The second rule was that he had no intention of totally abandoning Texas for Nashville, Tennessee. And the third edict was that—unfashionable as it seemed at the time—the cowboy hat was there to stay!

That first year in the recording business, George proudly announced to Nashville's *Music City News*, "If I find out later on that I have to move, well, I'll certainly move. But I would hate to leave Texas."[36]

With regard to the hat, he still recalls, "That's all I got when I came to town: 'Man, you sound great, but take the hat off, take the hat *off!*' "[37]

George made it clear that he was happy to keep his personal life just that—his personal life. He left Norma back in Texas when he went out on his first concert tours, where she could take care of their two young children: a daughter named Jenifer, and a son they named George,

Jr. To keep the two Georges in the family straight, they referred to the younger as "Bubba."

The second single released from George's debut album was "Down and Out," a bouncy ballad written by Dean Dillon and Frank Dycus. According to George, he preferred the song "If You're Thinking You Want a Stranger (There's One Coming Home)," and if it had been up to him, it should have been his second single. Instead, the record company chose to release "Down and Out." "Stranger," however, was destined to be his third single, released in January of 1982. On the country music charts it peaked at Number Three in *Billboard,* and at Number One in *Cash Box.* Suddenly the rush was on to get George back in the recording studio, to finish his follow-up album, *Strait from the Heart.*

The recording sessions for his second album reached as far back as September 9, 1981, when George laid down his vocals and basic tracks for "Fool Hearted Memory." It was destined to be the first song released as a single from his sophomore LP. It was also the first of his long string of singles to land at the top of *Billboard* magazine's Country Singles chart.

The album's masterpiece was a song that no one associated with George even dreamed he would find appealing. Since Strait had veered constantly toward traditional country tunes, the last thing anyone thought he would want to cut was a song about a lush port city in California. However, the second he heard the demo for "Marina Del Rey," he flipped out over it.

As George explains it, "I had done a show at Billy Bob's in Fort Worth, and Frank Dycus, who cowrote the song with Dean, had come to the show. He and his wife were going back down to San Marcos, where we lived, to spend a few days with us, and we were going to attempt to write some songs. Frank put the cassette in the player when we were going down the road, and I heard [the song], and he didn't really think it was the song for me. I'd just cut 'Unwound' and 'Down and Out,' and 'Marina Del Rey' was something that . . . well it was the first song on the tape."[38]

Frank was most amazed by George's fascination with the song, and his insistence that he be allowed to record it.

George surmised that Frank thought he was so "green" in the business that he couldn't hear an undeniable hit if it was anything short of swing or traditional country. George cut the song on January 11, 1982, at Music City Music Hall studios, with Blake Mevis producing.

In order to give the song a bit of atmosphere, Mevis ended the track with the faint sound of a bird tweeting in the background. From the very first time that he heard the finished song, George hated that damn bird, and insisted that it be exiled from the recording. Blake promised him that he would take the singing bird out, but he didn't. Strait insists to this day that he hates the ending to that song.

This song about California was destined to become one of George's most-requested signature songs. Erv Woolsey proudly points to that one tune as the song that really opened up everyone's eyes that George's singing potential was something more than a short-lived honky-tonk singer's. Most people didn't realize that he could really sing just about anything.

It was also on this second album that George took another stab at songwriting. "I Can't See Texas from Here" became the last time that he included any of his own compositions on his albums. He wrote the song in 1981 or 1982 as he was flying back to Texas from Nashville. It took him about ten minutes and was the last song he ever wrote. He believes he's had so much success with other song-writers that it's too hard for him to get motivated to write his own. The song is an amusing reply to everyone in Nashville asking him when he was going to move to

Tennessee. In the lyrics of the song, he answers with a chorus of the title, "I can't see Texas from here."

Another huge smash for George was "Amarillo by Morning," written by Terry Stafford and Paul Fraser. A warm ballad about the lonely life of a rodeo cowboy, out on the road, and longing for his lady in Amarillo, it shows Strait off as a perfect crooning balladeer. Bob Thompson's lonesome fiddle makes this song a memorable country classic.

Among the other highlights on George's *Strait from the Heart* is the up-tempo Guy C. Clark composition "Heartbroke." According to George, it was a much sought after song at the time. Ricky Skaggs had just cut the song about a month earlier, but George didn't know it at the time. He was opening a show for Skaggs somewhere on the road, and George did the song. As George watched, Skaggs told the audience he knew George had already done the song, but since it was his next single, he thought he'd sing it, too. Their versions were different, both live and on record. George's was a swing version, and Skagg's interpretation was more bluegrass.

George also cut his Texas songwriting buddy Darryl Staedtler's soulful "A Fire I Can't Put Out," and Clay Blaker's solemn song of losing everything but his true love. This album is much stronger and focused than its predecessor. Both "Amarillo by Morning" and "A Fire I Can't Put Out" were released as singles. "A Fire I Can't Put Out" became his second Number One hit in *Billboard*. Strait was clearly on a winning streak: during the years 1981 and 1982, there were seven George Strait singles released by MCA Records, and every one of them became Top Ten hits.

Listening to *Strait Country* and *Strait from the Heart* back-to-back, you can hear a difference in George's voice. On the second album he sounds much more relaxed and self-confident. In the first half of 1983 George went back in the studio with Blake Mevis. Together they cut eight new songs, including Hank Cochran and Dean Dillon's "What Would Your Memories Do." Somewhere amid that eighth session, George realized that his relationship with his producer was not working. He complained to Erv Woolsey, and a new producer was found.

George felt that the new material Mevis was having him cut was veering off course from the kind of songs he preferred to sing. George wasn't concerned whether or not his songs crossed over to the mainstream pop music charts, he was going to make the kind of music that *he* liked, and he was not going to be dictated to. He decided that he wanted to work with someone who had the traditional country sound under his belt. George chose Ray Baker for the task. Ray had worked with Merle Haggard, and George saw this as a big plus. He'd listened to the stuff Baker had done and thought it sounded great.

In defense of his move, George has explained that he felt like a record company was behind him, and that there was a market for good country music. It wasn't that the music wasn't good then, it just wasn't the kind of music that George particularly wanted to sing. He was the one who was going to have to sing it, and he felt that if he had cut songs he didn't believe in, and didn't like, he would just be wasting his time. He would be cheapening himself by not doing *his* music, by doing what somebody *else* wanted him to do.

Erv Woolsey's stance was that the problem between George and Blake was simply a matter of creative differences. After reviewing the eight new cuts, neither Erv nor George heard any obvious hit singles in the batch. Clearly it was the perfect time to make a change.

The album that resulted from the collaboration of Ray Baker and George Strait—*Right or Wrong*—was a huge success on several levels. Not only did this third album become his biggest hit yet, but it also produced three consecutive Number One singles. The first was the romantic ballad

"You Look So Good in Love," which was written by Rory Bourke, Glen Ballard, and Kerry Chater. For its release, MCA Records produced George's first video release. A slow-paced and romantic-themed video, George disliked it the minute he saw it. When it showed up on television, he absolutely cringed. He had them take it completely off the air because he wasn't happy with it. He felt it was embarrassing, corny, and syrupy. George maintains one of his biggest fears is to do another video like the first one. For a long time after that, he absolutely refused to do videos.

This is a typical George Strait move. There is no way that anyone can make him do what he doesn't want to do, and in an instance like this, there was no sense asking him. No one knew what was best for George other than George, and now that he was producing Number One singles, he was proving that *his* way of doing things was indeed the best way to proceed with his career.

The second Number One single from this album was "Right or Wrong," which was an old hit of Bob Wills & His Texas Playboys. Composed by Arthur L. Sizemore, Haven Gillespie, and Paul Biese, the up-tempo swing number was a song that George and Ace in the Hole had been playing in its live sets, and its transition to record was perfectly executed. This cut and this album feature the fiddle work of Johnny Gimble, who was one of the original Playboys. George was honored to have him on this album, and every one of his successive studio albums right up through *Holding My Own* in 1992.

Although romantic and a touch on the overly sweet side, the song "A Little Heaven's Rubbing Off on Me" is one of the album's catchiest and most memorable performances. Lush and slow, this song by John Scott Sherrill and Gene Dobbins pulled George into more of a pop context.

Shifting gears into rowdy honky-tonk mode came Darryl Staediler's raucous "80 Proof Bottle of Tear Stopper." The down-home feeling of the song proved quite infectious. It was a song that George had originally cut on his first trip to Nashville with Darryl Staedtler and Finlay. George had always fancied this song, and when it came time to pick material for the *Right or Wrong* album, this one came to mind. With its clever lyrics, and the performance that George delivered, it is one of the most fun cuts on the LP.

The third Number One single to be pulled from the album was "Let's Fall to Pieces Together." This was the first waltz that George Strait had ever recorded—with the exception of his old composition "(That Don't Change) The Way I Feel about You," which he had recorded for D Records. It remains one of George's favorite recordings.

Also on this album is the Merle Haggard song "Our Paths May Never Cross." A beautiful ballad about drifting through life without ever finding a soulmate, George makes this one of this album's zeniths. He got the opportunity to pay tribute to two of his idols on this disc.

Through his first three albums, George Strait was very quickly becoming the hot new country singer to watch. One reviewer even claimed that George was to country what James Taylor was to folk music. He had just racked up four consecutive Number One singles, and was on his way to a long and exciting career. However, he was beginning to recognize the frustrations of not feeling that he was in control of his own career. More changes for him were waiting right around the bend.

Chapter Five

"Something Special"

Through the incredibly appealing, expressive, yet simple music contained on his first three albums, George Strait very quickly established himself as one of the most important new singers in all of Nashville. He continued his insistence at keeping his music true to him, his voice and his personality. According to him, "Everywhere I go, people tell me, 'Keep it country—don't change it.' "[34] He was doing just that.

He had not only attracted legions of traditional country music fans, but he had also won the respect of his peers. According to John Anderson, it was Strait's sincerity that was the key to his success. "George is a real good, sincere person," said Anderson in 1984, "and it comes out in his music. If it didn't, he wouldn't have hits."[40]

No one was more amazed at his success than George was himself. The previous year when he had performed in concert with John Anderson and George Jones, he claimed, "I had to almost slap myself to make sure I wasn't dreamin'!"[41]

Following the current trends in modern country music, *Newsweek* magazine, in its January 9,1984, issue featured an article entitled "Country Purists Fight Back." In it, writer David Gates claimed, "George Strait and John Anderson are the hottest new properties in the country music counter-revolution begun by Ricky Skaggs a couple of years ago. At a time when the country music audience had reached an all-time high, the music's actual country content seemed to have hit rock bottom. A few uncompromising tradition-alists like Merle Haggard and George Jones refused to abandon the sobbing steel guitars, keening fiddles, biting guitar leads and the taut, passive singing in unashamedly Southern accents that characterize hard-core country music. Until recently, though, few new singers seemed interested in recreating this bittersweet sound or in run-ning the risk of alienating an increasingly unurbanzied and pop-oriented public."[42]

The year 1984 represented several major changes for George and for his manager, Erv Woolsey. Up until this point, George was still in embryonic stages of his career as a country star. A well-known hit maker, he was still a long way from the rarefied superstar stratosphere that he now exists in. *Billboard* magazine in February 1984 carried a piece about Strait and his Ace in the Hole band, which had grown from three to five musicians. The asking price to book them at a club or concert hall had increased to between $15,000 and $20,000 for a single performance.

Speaking of his newfound success during this time, George shrugged his shoulders and modestly surmised, "It seems pretty obvious that there's a shift back to more country-sounding records. I guess I'm in the right place at the right time."[43]

George was involved in the production of his fourth album for MCA in the beginning of the year, when major changes began to take place in his career. He and Ray

Baker had completed ten new tracks for LP number four, and plans were under way for its release later that year.

In April something happened that put the spotlight clearly on George's blossoming recording career. That month the Los Angeles-based Academy of Country Music awarded him the prestigious honor as their Male Vocalist of the Year. This not only signified the fact that his popularity had increased in leaps and bounds during the past three years since he had debuted on the charts, but it also meant that there were some truly strong expectations placed on his next MCA release.

The following month, in May 1984, a huge shake-up took place at MCA. Jim Fogelsong, who had originally inked Strait to his first recording deal, left MCA and was replaced by Jimmy Bowen as the head of the country music division of the record label. Bowen was known for making swift changes in personnel, and when he received this promotion at MCA, it was no exception. How did this affect George "Male Vocalist of the Year" Strait? Erv Woolsey received his pink slip at MCA and the ten tracks that George had recorded with Ray Baker were immediately scrapped.

While these events could be interpreted as catastrophic to Strait's career, in actuality, they turned up the intensity of it. The most interesting was Erv's firing. While at MCA the last three years, Erv had been overseeing George's fledgling career from within his post at the record company. Now, he was suddenly free to set up his own personal management company, and to concentrate on his number one concern: managing George's career. The head of MCA in New York City, Irving Azoff, had wanted to find Woolsey another post at MCA, but Erv saw this as the opportunity he had been waiting for. He established "The Erv Woolsey Company," and his offices officially opened on 18th Avenue South in Nashville. Now he was free to turn his full attention to George.

Erv chose to look at all of the positive sides to this new situation. He acknowledges Jimmy Bowen was a huge help in getting the Erv Woolsey Company started, and will always be grateful to him for it.

With regard to George's relationship to MCA Records, Jimmy Bowen suggested George fire Ray Baker and begin coproducing his albums with Bowen. Ray Baker had produced the *Right or Wrong* album, which was the first album to go Gold. But the opportunity to coproduce his own albums and have more control in the studio was too much for George to turn away.

He admitted that he and Ray Baker were not exactly seeing eye-to-eye in the recording studio anyway. "I don't know," he said in an attempt to pinpoint their differences in the studio. "It might have just been because of my nervousness in the studio, but when I was working with those other producers, I was a little bit afraid to put my own two cents' worth in. I would do it, ya know, but I always felt like maybe I was stepping out of line a little bit. But I know I *shouldn't* have felt like that, because it's *my* music that's going out there."[44]

He was beginning to feel that he had grown and developed a great deal in the last year, as a performer, and specifically as a recording artist. Ray had a certain way that he wanted to do things in the studio, and George was no longer feeling as intimidated in the studio as he had at first. His recording band was composed of musicians that had worked with great artists, and George had felt that his comments hadn't mattered.

The coproduction aspect wasn't something that George sought out. Jimmy Bowen offered him the opportunity to take more control over what he was doing in the studio, telling George the records were George's, not his, the sound was George's, not his, so George should be the one making the decisions.

Although, on the outside, it appeared to be a very gutsy

move, George asserted, "It's my career, it's my life. Who else can control it? You have to be in control of it."[45] With that, a whole new phase of his recording career began to unfold. George and Jimmy went into Sound Stage Studios in Nashville and began working on the album that ultimately was titled *Does Fort Worth Ever Cross Your Mind*. Strait made himself do a lot more work than he had ever thought about doing for a record before. He involved himself in the arrangements of the tunes, deciding where the instrumental parts would go.

George had complained in the past how in many instances, he had been told what songs he would or would not record. This was not the case with Jimmy. It was all done democratically. "Bowen and I met, and he really believed in me," says George of the album-mapping-out process that he went through with Bowen for the *Fort Worth* album. "He thought something was missing in my records. He came out and saw one of our shows and felt like my originality in concerts didn't come across on record. This time I really listened to a lot of songs and picked the material myself. I went around to all the major publishers and listened hard. Before, I had always been handed a list of songs my producer had picked out and I had to choose from those. Jimmy let me do pretty much what I wanted to do in the studio."[46]

George was absolutely thrilled at the way the actual recording process was unfolding. It wasn't a case of the musicians laying down their tracks, and then him coming in and recording his vocals. He said of Bowen's immeasurable assistance, "He would set up all the technical stuff and let me work with the musicians. This album reflects more of the way I hear the music because I talked to the musicians themselves. I didn't have to sit there and let the producer tell the guys how they think the songs should sound. I don't feel like I'm stepping out of line with Bowen if I say something. Before, I almost hated to say anything,

even if I felt strongly about something. Jimmy introduced
me to things in the studio I had never been exposed to.
I really respect him. I couldn't be happier. He said, 'You're
the one who has to sing the songs. It's your show.' "[47]
George was clearly on his way to his most creatively successful album.

Looking for specific songs for the album, Jimmy and
George stumbled on the song that was to become the
album's title cut and debut single. At Tree Publishing Company, Whitey Shafer was pitching a lot of songs, and sang
them himself. George fell in love with "Fort Worth" the
first time he heard it. The song made the album.

Another significant tune from that album is Sonny
Throckmorton and Casey Kelly's "The Cowboy Rides
Away." It immediately appealed to the cowpoke in George.
It is still a song that Strait performs in concert. Usually,
he ends his shows with this mid-tempo ode to the men
who ride horses, and how—when love goes bad—the cowboy rides off into the sunset alone. George has said that
at a concert, certain songs go over really, really well and
that this one gives a lot to a live show.

Another of the album's highlights is Mack Vickery and
Wayne Kemp's exciting ode to the men who drive the big
red trucks: "The Fireman." In this song—which is still a
huge country dance floor hit—the lyrics refer not to men
who extinguish towering infernos in houses and forests.
In this case, George sings of putting out the flames of love
affairs gone out of control. This exciting, fast-paced song
is another of George's personal favorites, which he gives
a red-hot treatment to whenever he performs it in concert.

Among the other exciting cuts on this album was the
perfect two-stepping sound of "Love Comes from the
Other Side of Town," and the slower-paced "Honky Tonk
Saturday Night." The whole album was instantly pleasing
for all of George's fans— both old and new—when it was
released in September 1984.

The following spring, in April 1985, his hard work paid off when the Academy of Country Music named *Does Fort Worth Ever Cross Your Mind* their Album of the Year. As if that wasn't enough, they repeated the previous year's honor by naming him their Male Vocalist of the Year.

Strait admitted that he was totally flabbergasted at the honor he received that night. He was so excited and surprised that he totally forgot to thank Jimmy Bowen when he got up on stage to accept the award. It wasn't until afterward that he realized what he had inadvertently done. Of hurting Bowen's feelings, George later lamented, "He never really said much about it, but I could tell that I'd really screwed up."[48]

In addition to the accolades, that same month, the *Does Fort Worth Ever Cross Your Mind* album was certified Gold for racking up over 500,000 copies sold. Since the sale of country music albums had cooled off in the mid-'80's, this was quite a feat. This brought his number of Gold albums to two . . . and growing.

Because of the awards, the record sales, and his increased radio airplay, George almost immediately began to see a transformation coming over his concert crowds. The response to his hits and his new material was increasing by the night. He was doing about two hundred concert dates per year, and was constantly on the road. He could see a change in the crowds, in the reaction of people to him when he did his shows.

To commemorate the end of George's first hit-making era, in March 1985, MCA released the first *George Strait: Greatest Hits* album. It was comprised entirely of cuts from his first three albums. From his work with Blake Mevis came the songs "Unwound," "Down and Out," "If You're Thinking You Want a Stranger (There's One Coming Home)," "Fool Hearted Memory," "Marina Del Rey," "Amarillo by Morning," and "A Fire I Can't Put Out." From his Ray Baker produced material came the three consecutive Number One hits: "You Look So Good in Love," "Right or Wrong," and "Let's Fall to Pieces Together."

The *George Strait: Greatest Hits* album is still on the *Billboard* magazine "Top Country Catalog Albums" as of 1996, and it has sold over two million copies. It continues to sell copies week after week, nearly a dozen years from its initial release.

In February 1985 George and Jimmy Bowen had already begun several days of intensive recording back at Sound Stage Studios in Nashville. He was on a winning streak, and his new material had to reflect the glories his career was racking up. In other words: ten more helpings of unadulterated George Strait.

George had assembled a strong cast of songwriting characters for himself on his 1985 *Something Special* album. His buddy Dean Dillon was represented here by a pair of his songs: "You Sure Got This Ol' Redneck Feelin' Blue" written with Buzz Rabin, and "The Chair" written with Hank Cochran. Also on the album was Harlan Howard, who with Shirl Milete wrote "I've Seen That Look on Me (A Thousand Times)." This is significant because both Hank and Harlan were two of country legend Patsy Cline's favorite songwriting pals back in the early 1960s. Hank had given Patsy "She's Got You" (1961), "Why Can't He Be You" (1962) and "When You Need a Laugh" (1962). Harlan wrote "That's How a Heartache Begins" (1962), "He Called Me Baby" (1962), and "You Took Him off My Hands" (1963). As a team, it was Harlan Howard and Hank Cochran who penned Patsy's immortal "I Fall to Pieces" (1960). In Nashville terms, to have two heavyweights like Cochran and Howard contributing songs to your new album was major league.

George is the first to admit that a major reason for the great success that his sixth album, *Something Special,* enjoyed was directly related to the varied and strong songs he and

Jimmy found for it. The album had a lot of quality material and included "You're So Special," "Haven't You Heard," "In Too Deep," "You Sure Got This Ol' Redneck Feelin' Blue," "The Chair," and "Lefty's Gone."

The title cut of the *Something Special* album was written by David Anthony, who plays rhythm guitar and sings in George's band. He had written the song back when he was with Reba McEntire's band. George and Reba had been doing a show together somewhere in Florida soon after David had demoed his song. He went on George's bus and played it for him. It had the slow swing George liked.

According to George, one of his favorite songs on the album was the old lamenting tune "Haven't You Heard." A quirky and lonesome tune, the song has lyrics about mama running off, and daddy going crazy. Strait was later to explain that his father wasn't at all happy about his son singing this song. It hit a little too close to home for his father to appreciate it as a song. This is perhaps the frankest that George Strait has ever been about the never-talked-about exit of his mother from his own life, over twenty years before.

The song "Lefty's Gone," by Sanger D. "Whitey" Shafer, is about the death of country legend Lefty Frizzell. Whitey played George the demo for the song at the same time that he presented him with "Does Fort Worth Ever Cross Your Mind." Whitey and Lefty Frizzell had been very close buddies, and this was a tribute to his fallen friend. George recalls that Whitey had written the song so very much from his heart that he had to leave the room when George listened to the demo tape. The song had seemed to haunt him over the last year, and he decided to record it for this album.

The fall of 1985 seemed to belong to George Strait. The first single from the new album was released in August of that year, and it jumped up the country music charts to become his seventh Number One hit single in *Billboard*.

The following month, his new *Something Special* album was released, and immediately became a hit. In October the Country Music Association concurred with the Academy of Country Music, and George won the CMA award as Male Vocalist of the Year, and *Does Fort Worth Ever Cross Your Mind* took the Album of the Year honors.

As 1985 came to a close, everything was going great for George. He was very comfortable and settled in his relationship with his new producer. "Jimmy Bowen's just great," Strait explained of their working relationship in the mid-'80s. "It's funny the way we coproduce an album, because I don't think anybody else does it quite like this. I go in the studio and I can do my part in four or five days—cut the basic tracks, do my vocals. Then we'll go over the different songs, and we'll decide where we want harmony parts, and how many, and this and that. And I'll go on home to Texas or whatever, and he'll go back in the studio and do 'em. Then he'll send me all these cassette tapes of what he's done, and I'll listen to them and call him up and say 'yes' to this, or 'no' to that, or 'this sounds great,' or 'Let's change this to this,' or 'Let's cut this part out.' Jimmy will go back in the studio and make all the changes, then send me another cassette of it to listen to. He'll send me maybe twenty cassettes before we finally get through. I'm really serious about my music. Every time I go in the studio to make a new record, I get nervous because I want it to be my best ever. Not really different, but just *better,* because I hope to be doing this same thing for years to come."[49]

George's concert tour schedule was getting more and more hectic by the month. Explaining his drive to *People* magazine that year, he said, "I'd be crazy to slow down right now; things are going too good. I have to hit it full steam until I can't stand it anymore."[50]

His devoted wife Norma admitted, "He hates being gone so much. He says if he could make that much money and not travel so much, he would.''[51] It costs a lot of money to pay the salaries of the band, have a ranch tucked away in mid-Texas, record a new hit album a year, and do as many concerts as possible.

One of the things that really affected George was the unwavering devotion that he felt from his strongest and most devoted fans. He couldn't understand how he could see some fans in Texas one night, and then the next night see them again in another state. He and the band had to drive nonstop all night and day to get to the next concert on time. Realizing his fans had done the same thing was very flattering.

In spite of all of his fame, success and the degree of adulation that he felt from his public, George still claimed in 1985 that he didn't really feel he had made it yet. He wanted to be in the Country Music Hall of Fame.

Chapter Six

"Triumph & Tragedy"

When George Strait won his Country Music Association awards in the fall of 1985, the headline in Nashville's *Music City News* was " '85 CMA Award: A Return to Tradition." According to the article, "Country's 'new traditionalists' stole the show at last month's Country Music Association Awards, with Ricky Skaggs, George Strait, Reba McEntire and The Judds taking top honors in a combined total of seven different categories. . . . Soft-spoken, cowboy-hatted George Strait landed two major honors."[52]

At this point in time the division widened between the new traditionalist country music and the pop/country music John Schneider, Juice Newton, Crystal Gayle, Donna Fargo, Eddie Rabbitt and others were placing on the charts. George and Reba were really leading the way back to pure country. Reba has since veered back to pop, but at the time she was classified as a new traditionalist. George has remained unwavering about his convictions to his music.

He and Reba were so closely aligned in musical taste in 1985-1986, that there was constant talk about them recording a song together. According to George at the time, "She and I have talked about doing a duet before, but whether we'll ever get the time to do it. You gotta find the material: it just takes a lot of time, and she's real busy and I'm real busy. I just don't know. I'm not gonna say we're not gonna do one, but it's not in the real near future."[53] To date it has not yet happened.

The debate between the new traditionalists and the pop/country singers was heating up in 1986. When dragged into the fray that year, George replied, "Everybody has to ask me about that, but I really hate to get into it. Yeah, there's more traditional-type country around than there was seven or eight years ago, and I hope that continues. I'm a country singer, but when I'm looking for songs to do, I don't go out with a specific kind of song in mind. I just look for a *good song*. Whether it's traditional or contemporary doesn't matter to me; if I hear it and I like it, I can do it the way I want to do it. I mean, 'Marina Del Rey' and 'The Chair'—to me, those aren't traditional hardcore country-sounding records; but I feel like they're good songs, and they were good for me. That's why I did them."[54]

In May 1986 George released his next album, appropriately entitled #7, the third consecutive album he coproduced with Jimmy Bowen. His new holiday album was already planned for later that year. Of his growing consistency, George said at the time that #7 had a bunch of new songs, but there wasn't anything radically different. He was looking forward to doing the Christmas album, which would have some old standards and some new Christmas songs.

On the #7 album, George discovered eight new songs that he really enjoyed, and dug into the songbooks of two of his idols for a couple of classics. Out of the Tex Ritter songbook came the downhome charm of "Cow Town." From his Texas swing hero, Bob Wills, he recorded "Deep Water," which had originally been recorded by Wills and

His Texas Playboys. Ex-Playboy Johnny Gimble was on hand in the recording studio to add his authentic fiddle playing to George's treatment of the song. Speaking about where he found his songs for this album, he replied at the time, "Oh, the same place I find everything else. I just go look for them here and there. I go to publishing houses, people send me stuff; whenever I get to Nashville I've got a big box full to the top with tapes that I have to go through."[55]

He further explained, "I look constantly for songs. We get tapes on the road a lot. I've got some people in Texas that I go through their stuff—some real good songwriters. We find 'em where I can get 'em."[56]

So far, his instincts all seemed to be holding true. No one put any pressure on him about his material, but he was sure that if he took a rotten song into the studio, Jimmy Bowen wouldn't hesitate to tell him not to do it. George trusted Jimmy's taste.

He surmised that only George Strait could effectively pick out songs for George Strait. It would be like buying shoes for a friend. If he wasn't there with you, you could never be sure of the fit. No one could pick songs for an artist better than the artist himself.

George was so enamored of the Bob Wills number that he recorded for his seventh album, that he seriously contemplated recording an all Bob Wills album. In 1993, Asleep at the Wheel beat him to the punch. Said George back in 1986, "I've thought about doing a swing album. It'd be something that I'd really like to do. If Haggard hadn't done it, I'd like to do a tribute album to [Bob] Wills, but after Hag does something, you can't hardly make it much better. So if the time ever comes around [to] where I'm able to do an album of all swing, then I'd like to do it."[57]

While the traditional country vs. pop/rock/country war was raging, the rock & roll bi-monthly bible *Rolling Stone* gave #7 its most glowing review. According to reviewer

James Hunter, "Forget George Strait as the white-Stetsoned sheriff of country's current 'new traditionalism.' Think of him instead as Elvis Presley balladeering out of the Lone Star State, with hardly a sneer or demon in sight ... On #7 ... there are three blue-chip songs on his record that show Strait for what he plainly is: one of the two or three finest country singers of his generation." Hunter went on to point out those three stellar songs as being "Nobody in His Right Mind Would've Left Her," "It Ain't Cool to Be Crazy about You," and "Stranger Things Have Happened." The review ended with the fitting opinion, "For the past couple of years, Strait has acted as though rock & roll never unwound. But he doesn't sacrifice much cool, not yet anyway. He's no sheriff; he's a swinger."[58]

On the perfectly balanced and crisp-sounding album, George proved song after song that #7 was indeed a lucky number. "Nobody in His Right Mind Would've Left Her," by Dean Dillon, was a song that George had originally recorded the first time he traveled to Nashville to record with Blake Mevis. He had cut it along with "The Perfect Lie," and "Blame it on Mexico." It was a song that George had always loved, and it seemed to have haunted him the last five years. Finally he decided to include it on this album. It was a stroke of perfect instinct, as "Nobody in His Right Mind Would've Left Her" was destined to become his eighth Number One single when it was released in the spring of 1986.

Likewise, with "It Ain't Cool to Be Crazy about You." It is a perfect song that George Strait was to take all the way up the charts to Number One.

Also on this album is George's version of the David Chamberlain song "Stranger Things Have Happened." He briefly returns to the fireman image on the two-stepping tempo "My Old Flame Is Burnin' Another Honky Tonk Down." This time around, instead of putting out the fires, he simply follows his ex-lover's trail of pyromania from nightspot to nightspot. All in all, #7 was George's finest album to date.

That spring, George went into the recording studio with classic Nashville performer Hank Thompson and cut a duet version of the song "Six Pack to Go," which had originally appeared on one of Hank's albums. George had been doing this song in his show for a long time, and he'd always admired Hank Thompson. Thompson did great songs, including a lot of swing. George had met him in Oklahoma, and they had become friends. Hank was doing an album of his old songs, and he asked George if he'd do "Six Pack to Go" with him as a duet. George was happy to comply.

Everything was going fabulously for George Strait at the start of 1986. No one was more thankful than he for all of the success and wonderful people who surrounded him. "I feel real blessed to be where I am," he said at the time. "I'm not about to give it up. There's been talk about movies and TV and stuff, but I'm pretty much involved in the country music business. My record company has its own ideas about this, but my opinion is that when actors and singers try to trade roles, ninety percent of the time it doesn't work. There are exceptions, of course, but not many. So I'm happy singing country music, and I would be happy if I never did a picture in my whole life. There's nothing wrong with branching out, but you can't let go of the thing that made you. I'm gonna be a country singer 'til I die."[59]

After struggling with the uncomfortable aspects of fame for several years, he was finally relaxing into it. "I'm handling it pretty well," he claimed. "You see, it's wonderful. It's what everybody who's starting out in the music business is trying to get to, and I'll tell you: it really is as good as you think it's going to be. I *love* it. I can handle a *lot* of it. It is great, don't get me wrong, but there's a lot more work to it than I realized. Anybody who gets in this situation finds that out. There's a lot of work that people don't know about, but you have to do a lot of long, long hours. A lot of people making demands on you."[60]

Back home in Texas, his wife, Norma, and his two children, thirteen-year-old Jenifer and five-year-old Bubba were leading normal lives while daddy was out on the road entertaining his fans.

Speaking about the strain that his career had taken on his marriage from 1981 to 1986, George explained Norma's stance, "Right at first, it was real hard, a hard adjustment to make. She used to travel with me quite a bit, but there just isn't anything on the road for [her] to do. It just gets old unless you're like me: I'm out there working. So that got old to her. We've got two kids. During the school year it's almost impossible for her to go 'cause my little boy is just fixing to turn five in May, and he'll be starting preschool or kindergarten or whatever you call it next year. My daughter's thirteen, so she's got interests at home there, people that she wants to be with—her friends. So, she really doesn't care anything about going out on the road, plus she can't during the school year. I think we've adjusted as well as anybody can: it's working real good right now. Course it's just like any other marriage, y'know? There's the good times and the bad times. I don't feel like me bein' in the position that I'm in right now. I don't think that it makes it that much worse. We've adjusted to it, in other words."[61]

On June 25, 1986, something terrible happened. George and Norma's young daughter Jenifer was killed in a car accident. The exact circumstances surrounding the accident are rarely discussed. The loss was painfully deep.

According to David Daily, "The only thing that I heard was that she was coming home from a friend of hers' house. I believe that it was her and another girl, and I think a teenage boy was driving them. . . . They were coming home and, I don't know if they were going around a corner or what, but he lost control of the car and it flipped into a ditch, and I think she got thrown out of the car. That's really about all I know. I don't know what the situation was, or exactly who was driving, or what, but he was probably just a young teenager who was hot-rodding and probably showing off. That's about what I figure. It was real sad, and a real scary deal. I couldn't help but wonder what was going to happen to George, whether he was going to sing again, or what. I guess he just decided to go on and continue doing what he does—which is probably the best thing, rather than just sitting around thinking about it. He decided to just get out and stay busy. And that's exactly what he did and it seems to have worked out for him."

True to form for George, he withdrew from the public. There were no public statements made by him, and it became a completely avoided topic of discussion in all interviews for several years. Only recently has George been able to even discuss it on any level. In 1995 in the *Journal Of Country Music* George stated, "Early in my career, I had a very tragic thing happen. And I just realized that, you know, nothing could be worse than that. And so I'm gonna make these decisions, and if they're right, they're right. If they're wrong, so be it. That's the way it's gonna be. And so, that's what I've done. I'm sure I may have made a lot of people mad, I don't know. But that's the way I chose to do it, and lucky for me it hasn't hurt my career any."[62]

What George did to work his way through his pain was to bury himself in his work. Although it was hard to remain joyful about it, he recorded his Christmas album right on schedule that summer, for September release, and he returned to his concert work.

To listen to the *Merry Christmas Strait to You* album, you wouldn't have a clue that the man singing a jovial Nashville version of "Frosty the Snowman" and an anticipatory "Santa Claus Is Coming to Town," is amid the throes of emotional pain. Bob Kelly penned the clever title cut,

"Merry Christmas Strait to You," and Hank Cochran and Harlan Howard brought him "What a Merry Christmas This Could Be." For the right bit of country flavor, George used Keith Whitley's "There's a New Kid in Town." Dean Dillon and Hank Cochran had fun with the somber and beautiful "For Christ's Sake, It's Christmas." Benny McArthur's "When It's Christmas Time in Texas" provided George with the most swinging song on the album. It still continues to be a December favorite album for country music fans a decade after its initial release.

On his emotional recovery trail, in 1986 George went on to break the attendance record at Atlanta's Omni Auditorium, selling seventeen thousand seats in an amazing forty-five minutes. Then he went on and sold out San Antonio's fifteen thousand-seat Freeman Auditorium.

With regard to that last feat, George proclaimed, "Well, Texas has always been really good for me, ever since 'Unwound' came out. I grew up real close to San Antone, and that part of the country is like home to me. I have a lot of friends there, and fifteen thousand of 'em showed up that night."[63]

That October, George again won the Vocalist of the Year Award from the Country Music Association. Although he never publicly addressed his painful loss, when he took the podium to accept his award, he dedicated it to Jenifer's memory.

At this point, George had already begun completing the recording of his ninth album, *Ocean Front Property*. The most extensive recording had taken place September 23–30, yielding such gems as "Am I Blue," "Second Chances," and the enormously appealing "All My Ex's Live in Texas."

On one hand, 1986 had been a horrifying ordeal of grief for George; however, on the career side, it had been brilliantly successful for him. Both the *Something Special* and the #7 albums had been certified Gold during the year, and he had racked up another pair of Number One hit singles. The only way for George to move was forward, and that is just what he did.

To keep the pace moving, he finished off 1986 busier than ever. He performed at Dallas' Reunion Arena on New Year's Eve. The show, with its wildly enthusiastic crowd, was taped in its entirety, and was to be released as a video cassette, *George Strait Live,* the following year.

The year 1987 began with a bang for George. When the tickets for his upcoming concert performance at Houston's massive Astrodome went on sale January 6, they sold out in twenty-four hours. When the figures were totaled, he had sold 49,246 seats for the February 25 concert appearance. The two-night engagement sold the astonishing number of 112,808 tickets. You might say that he was a Strait sensation in Texas!

This was an indication that George was more than a regional Texas sensation. People were slow to abandon the regional label, but he was selling in a lot of other places, not just in Texas. George and his band were drawing great crowds and were a great success.

With regard to those two record-breaking dates in Houston, George found them exhilarating. "I can't put it into words what it feels like to play a place that big!" he said. "You can't see the audience, but you can hear them; you can *feel* the energy! Boy, I get nervous before a show like that! I mean, we're maybe up there for an hour and a half, but after we're through, I'm all hyped up for hours and hours. Then when I finally do settle down, I feel *exhausted!* Drained! Like I'd been up onstage for eight hours or something!"[64]

When the album *Ocean Front Property* was released in January, it became the first album to ever debut at Number One on *Billboard* magazine's Country Albums chart. George was just making and breaking records right and left.

The title cut, "Ocean Front Property," was the first single from the album. Written by Dean Dillon, Hank Cochran, and Royce Porter, the song is about giving an old lover the kiss off. It became the first of three consecutive Number One singles from the album. The next one to pole-vault up the charts was "All My Ex's Live in Texas." It was written by Whitey Shafer and Lyndia Shafer. George has always believed it was a true story about Whitey and thinks a lot of Whitey's songs were true stories. At the time, George was trying to make sure he put a little bit of swing on each album. This was in the swing vein, and it had some good instrumentation on it. The song was nominated for a Grammy. George went to the Grammy Awards and performed it.

David Chamberlain's composition "Am I Blue," a percolating slice of true country, complete with steel guitars and fiddles, became the third chart-topping single from the *Ocean Front Property* album. Swinging and moderately up-tempo in pace, George sounds great on this cut that is reminiscent of something that would have been featured in a Bob Wills & His Texas Playboys concert twenty years earlier.

Another unique thing about this album is that it features the recording debut of the Ace in the Hole band. George's touring band, which was now up to an eight-piece ensemble, can be heard on the songs "Hot Burning Flames" and "You Can't Buy Your Way Out of the Blues."

"I can't say enough good things about my band," George explained. "I think they are the best band on the road out there today, and have been for a long time. I'll put them up against anybody out there at a concert, and there's no question they can play their butts off in the studio, too. But it's just the fact that it's easier for me to go in the studio with session musicians, and it's a lot faster for me."[65]

In other words, it was much easier for him to book people in Nashville whose sole job was playing for recording sessions than it was to juggle the schedules of his regular band members. There was also the expense of flying the band there, booking the studio, etc. Efficiency matters to George Strait. It is, however, a treat to hear Ace in the Hole strutting themselves on a record.

In September 1987 a new George Strait album was in the record stores: *George Strait: Greatest Hits Volume Two*. This tenth LP reprised the greatest highlights of the singer's work since he had begun coproducing his recordings with Jimmy Bowen. It included "Does Fort Worth Ever Cross Your Mind," "The Cowboy Rides Away," "The Fireman," "The Chair," "You're Something Special to Me," "Nobody in His Right Mind Would've Left Her," "It Ain't Cool to Be Crazy about You," "Ocean Front Property," "All My Ex's Live in Texas," and "Am I Blue."

Just like its predecessor, *George Strait: Greatest Hits, George Strait: Greatest Hits Volume Two* has gone on to sell over two million copies, and is still in the Top Ten on the *Billboard* Country Catalog Albums chart as of 1996.

After the car accident that claimed Jenifer, George began to cut back on the tour dates, to spend more quality time with his family. According to him, "There was a time when I was playing 220 dates a year. I hardly ever got to see my family, and I wondered if I could do it again another year. But I'd take some time off at the ranch in October or November, do a little hunting and fishing and be ready to go again. We're doing fewer dates a year now, but we're playing in bigger arenas so we can still reach as many fans. Still, it's darned nice to get home."[66]

Another of George's 1987 feats came when he became the first performer since Elvis Presley to sell out his debut engagement at the Hilton Hotel casino in Las Vegas. Among the people in the audience that night was Colonel Tom Parker, the legendary and controversial manager of Elvis Presley. During this engagement George and the Colonel struck up a nice friendship. George was to explain not long afterward, "It was pretty neat meeting him. He gave us a few pointers in the movie business."[67] A liaison was to develop in time. In George, Parker saw the kind of magic that Elvis had possessed. He was later to hold the key to one of George's greatest successes.

As 1987 came to an end, George had an impressive list of successes that he had tallied up in the past twelve months. Two new hit albums, three Number One singles, a best-selling video cassette, and record-breaking concert engagements. The healing process was well under way. Although he had been dealt a horrendous personal tragedy to survive, survive he would, and emerge from it stronger than ever.

Chapter Seven

"Livin' It Up"

The last three years of the decade found George in full form, pumping out three new albums, and his first video cassette. The in-concert videotape, *George Strait Live*, fittingly threw his white cowboy hat into that ring in 1987. George told *Billboard* magazine's Gerry Wood, "Videos in country music can be good if you want to take the time and spend the money and really do something different. If the story is there and you've got a good idea and can make it come off on tape, then it's great. If not, they're terrible."[68]

The *George Strait Live* video cassette sold in excess of fifty thousand copies by that summer—certifying it Gold—and since that time has nearly tripled that sales figure. When *Country Music* magazine reviewed it, critic Rich Kienzle proclaimed, "He tears through sixteen numbers—not all of his big hits, but a substantial chunk of what put him where he is today, showing clearly why he's one of the best entertainers the industry's seen in years . . . Strait's energy never lets up . . . The Ace in the Hole band is as awesome as you'd expect, with the twin fiddles of Benny McArthur and Gene Elders particularly outstanding."[69]

He still refused to do big dramatic acting videos like the ones that all of his contemporaries, such as Reba McEntire and Randy Travis, were doing at the time. He reiterated, "Well, we did *You Look So Good in Love.* I didn't like that video at all. I didn't like it when it was finished. That kind of soured me on videos. *Amarillo by Morning,* they took from the Houston rodeo and edited rodeo scenes in it. I kinda made up my mind if I was going to do another video, I wanted it to be a kinda 'live' band-type deal, so that's what we did when we did *The Chair.* I didn't mind doing that one as bad as I did *You Look So Good in Love,* but still it's not my favorite thing to do. I'm always glad after I finish doing 'em. Except that one. I had a talk recently with Irving Azoff [president of MCA Records], and he seems to think they're important, so I guess I'll be doing more."[70]

In the beginning of 1988, George was up for a Grammy Award for the song "All My Ex's Live in Texas," in the category of Best Country Vocal Performance, Male. Although George had a ball performing the song on the international telecast, Randy Travis' "Always & Forever" ended up with the gramophone-shaped trophy.

February 1988 saw the arrival of George's next album, *If You Ain't Lovin' (You Ain't Livin').* He continued to produce one Gold album after another in 1988,1989, and 1990. This was to represent another high water period for George, as he trajectorized eight more Number One singles to the top of *Billboard* magazine's country singles chart. It seemed like George Strait could do no wrong these three years. He was the hottest thing in Nashville, and everyone knew it.

From the very start of this album there is a sense that every song on it crackles with super-tight music, and there's a magically lighthearted excitement to George's vocals. He had established a winning formula for himself, and during these particular years, he showed off the fact that he had perfected it, refined and brought the record-buying public around to his way of thinking.

The title cut of Strait's eleventh album, *If You Ain't Lovin' (You Ain't Livin')* was written by Tommy Collins, and years earlier it had been recorded by country great Faron Young. George thought it was a neat, honky-tonking kind of song with a Hank Williams kind of sound. Young's version had been pitched to George, and he knew that type of song was hard to find, the good songs that hadn't been big records everybody remembered right away. It's tough to recut an old song and make it different.

The lullaby "Baby Blue" was the first song of Aaron Barker's that George Strait had recorded. Barker would later contribute several of George's most memorable hits, including "Love Without End, Amen" and "Easy Come, Easy Go" (with Dean Dillon). Erv Woolsey had met Aaron in Texas where he was writing songs for a small company in Hondo. George was instrumental in moving Aaron to Nashville where he now writes for Strait's publishing company. He claims that Aaron's original demo was so good that it was a hard act to follow.

According to George, "Famous Last Words of a Fool" was a tune that nearly never got recorded. He had passed on the song the album before, and Dean decided to pitch it to him again. The second time hit George right.

"If You Ain't Lovin' (You Ain't Livin')," "Baby Blue," and "Famous Last Words of a Fool" were all released as singles, and all of them promptly hit Number One. George was still on a "strait" winning streak that wouldn't stop.

The *If You Ain't Lovin', You Ain't Livin'* album also contained Ronnie McDowell's lamenting "Under These Conditions," the swinging David Chamberlain cut "It's Too Late Now," and L. David Lewis' ode to no-nonsense love: "Let's Get Down to It." Another smash release for George, it was certified Gold in April. That same month, George again took the Academy of Country Music's award as the Male Vocalist of the Year, further strengthening his stake as the hottest male performer in country music.

Throughout the bulk of the year, he was on tour with Marlboro tobacco sponsoring. Along the way, George found himself defending the fact that his tour was presented by Marlboro. Although he was a non-smoker, some people felt he was promoting cancer-causing cigarette smoking to his fans. "Well, I never really thought of it that way," he pondered, "that they were using me to sell cigarettes. I think it's more of an advantage to the country music fan than anything, because the ticket prices are so low, and they have sometimes four name acts on the same bill. And, you know, the seats are great, they have big screens, and they really don't try to shove anything about cigarettes or any of that promotion stuff down my throat. And it's really a professionally done tour, and as far as smokin', I don't smoke, and they know that, and I don't like people to smoke on my bus. But it's not a problem. They're promotin' country music, and if it happens to help the Marlboro name, well, that's their idea. But it's not a tour to go out and promote smokin' cigarettes."[71]

In 1988 George set a new record by selling over $10 million in concert ticket sales. His list of accomplishments continued to mount, triumph by triumph. Cigarettes or not, he was one smokin' act that year.

February 1989 saw the debut of George's *Beyond the Blue Neon* album. This album represented some changes and improvements that had Strait proclaiming, "I think this is the best album I've ever done, and it's real country. That material is really strong, and I'm having a hard time choosing singles, because I like every song on the album—and that's kind of unusual. You start out that way, normally, and when you get finished, there's always a few that stand out and sometimes a few that you don't do onstage. But we're going to do every one of these songs onstage, so I feel like I finally achieved what I was trying to achieve in the studio with this album."[72] "I felt excited when I came out of the studio, like I'd accomplished something I'd wanted to accomplish for a long, long time."[73]

According to George, the new twist came with the addition of a new instrument. He added a sax player to the studio band. Not for a saxophone solo, but simply to beef up the sound a little. He used the sax on some of the songs, and thought it worked really well.

The album opens with the swaying tempo of the title cut, written by Paul Nelson and Larry Boone. Conjuring the visions of a tavern where people go to drown their sorrows in a cocktail, George sounds excellent on this finely crafted album. One of the prime highlights comes on the amusing song "Hollywood Squares," which plays on the punlike parallels between "ex's" and the money he "owes," contrasted with the "Xs" and "Os" used to play the tic-tac-toe television gameshow of the same name.

"Baby's Gotten Good at Goodbye" came to him in a fluke. He had been trying unsuccessfully to record one of Dean Dillon's songs, and it just wasn't working out right. At the very end of the recording sessions for the album, George suddenly had to find another tune. Although this was written by Tony and Troy Martin, Dean had suggested it. It was the last song George cut in the studio for this album, and it turned out to be the best song on the album. Tony and Troy had never had a song of theirs cut before this one, and it ended up being the first of three Number One hit singles to be pulled from the album.

George's next chart-topping single came with "What's Going On in Your World." It had an old-fashioned traditional sound to it that appealed to George. David Chamberlain has a very unusual style of singing that came across really well on the demo. George's fans fell in love with George's version.

Dennis Adkins' composition, "Ace in the Hole" was almost too perfect for words, with a title that was the name of George's touring band. George had been pitched a few songs with this type of title before, but none had the right kind of swing. He felt the band should have a catchy little number to do, one that was a lot of fun. They did this song in Gruene Hall for a commercial.

Oddly enough, this was not a song that George cut with the Ace in the Hole band, despite its seeming such an obviously tailormade move. He admitted in retrospect that he caught a little flak on not bringing his band in to cut it. At the time, however, everyone's schedules just weren't right for it to happen.

The song ended up being one of the favorites for the band to really cook with while in concert. George loves giving them a chance to shine whenever he performs. "I've got a great band, so why not let 'em play?!" he exclaims. "It's fun to get up there and not only play the records, but to do some other stuff, as well; it's sometimes kind of off-the-wall, you know. I *love* the big band sound. You get such a full sound up onstage with that many players. If I could, I'd add more—a third fiddle player, probably a mandolin player, and maybe even some horns—like [Bob] Wills had."[74]

In the autumn of 1989, George won the Country Music Association's Entertainer of the Year Award. It was a real thrill to him, especially since he had been nominated for that award five times previously, and had never won it. "I *really* wanted that thing," he admitted, "and I was just about to think that it was gonna slip by me. It just knocked me out when they called my name! It's just one of those things that everybody in this business wants to get."[75]

Amid all of this activity, for George, one of the most exciting aspects of 1989 was his visit to the White House in Washington D.C. to meet President George Bush. He was there for a ceremony to honor people with vocational-technological educations who had become successful. George was impressed that the president knew all about him, including that he was from Poteet, Texas.

Honored along with George that day were General Joe Henry Eagle, fashion designer Norma Kamali, Delbert Staley, and Ralph Hofstad.

George, Norma, and George, Jr., were later asked to join the president in the Oval Office. As George, Jr., had taken a day off from school to attend the ceremonies, the president wrote a note explaining his absence and signed it. President Bush showed George a special office with a desk some friends had built for him. The desk had speakers built into it, and country music was playing.

George was thrilled to be receiving the honor that he did that day: "The award really meant a lot, especially coming from the president. I hope it can serve as an inspiration for some kids out there in high school and even younger that the 4H and FFA are really really good for young kids. I was in FFA in high school. It taught me a whole lot. I really enjoyed it. I love being outside, being around animals."[76]

George and President Bush, a fellow Texan, reportedly hit it off quite well, and he was asked to socialize with the president in a more informal setting. George, Norma, and George, Jr., were invited to Camp David to spend the weekend with President and Mrs. Bush. Bush asked George to do a small set for a few of their friends and guests at Camp David. George took along his guitar player and his piano player to perform before about thirty or forty people. It was at the same time as the Desert Storm conflict, so the president didn't get to enjoy the full concert as he was often called out of the room.

Reportedly, the president's favorite George Strait song is "Love Without End, Amen." George found the Bushes to be very charming and friendly. He even went jogging about two miles with the president. Although he was unused to jogging, Strait managed to keep up.

George Strait ended the decade of the '80s on top of the world. What could he possibly do in the new decade to top all of this? Looking back at the year 1989 at the end of it, George has admitted it was one of the greatest years he'd ever had. He received the Entertainer of the Year Award, which he'd really wanted, and it provided a needed boost for him. He'd been on the road for eight years, working hard, and the recognition gave him a shot in the arm. He was very proud of the honor and felt that even if he never won it again, he had gotten it once, and that was what mattered.

George was nothing but thankful and humble about all that he had accomplished between 1981 and 1989. It had been quite the decade for him, and he knew it. "I've achieved more than I ever thought I would," he said modestly. "I feel like I've been real lucky. When I first signed with MCA, there were a lot of big stars on the label— Haggard, Loretta, Tanya—and everybody was really hot. I figured, 'Well, yeah, I'm gonna sign, and my record is going to come out and get kind of slid underneath everything.' But that never happened. MCA always pushed me and the records, and I'm real thankful for that. But, we've also worked real hard, and it's not as easy as people think— being out there on the road a lot, as much as we are. But, I'm real thankful to be doing this, because there's not a lot of people who get to experience this. There are a lot of singers and musicians out there, but there's not many of them that get to really experience the music business like we are right now. So I'm real proud of that. That's something if you had asked me about ten years ago, I would have said, 'I doubt I'll ever get this far; but hopefully someday, I'll get a record on the radio.' "[77]

His final engagement for 1989 was a booking in Las Vegas. George was ready to wind it up for the year. He felt

Vegas was a great town, but a really difficult place to work—
harder for him than just about anywhere else. The rooms
he performed in were too small for him to be comfortable
performing.

Speaking of his hectic life on the road, George explained
at the time, "Out here you've really gotta pace yourself.
Especially if you're like me and you like to go out and take
part in what Las Vegas has to offer. If you don't, you'll
wear yourself out. This is the last show I have this year,
except for a New Year's Eve show in Houston. Then, after
the first of the year, I'll start my next album. I was supposed
to go in the studio in October, but this past summer we
ended up probably working more dates than we ever have
in one summer. I don't know how it happened, or why.
But it did. And I was just totally burned out and just needed
to get away some place and rest. So we postponed the
studio sessions until February, when maybe I'll feel a little
better."[78]

George had no trouble swinging right into the 1990s
with style and panache. In February of that year, George
was up in Nashville, at Emerald recording studio, working
on his thirteenth album, *Livin' It Up*. He simply took the
winning musical formula of *Beyond the Blue Neon* and magnified it. This time around, it was Jim Horn who took over
the sax duties in the recording studio. Also of special note
on this album are two more performances with George
backed by Ace in the Hole, on the cuts "Someone Had to
Teach You" and "She Loves Me (She Don't Love You)."

In April 1990, on the network television telecast of the
Academy of Country Music Awards, George introduced
the first single from the album, the heartfelt "Love Without
End, Amen." The song about a father's undying love for
his young son is a song that produces a lump in the throat,
and brings tears to the eyes. To really personalize the song,
George changed one of the lyrics to spotlight 1981, the
year that his son Bubba was born. It was an instant smash

when it was released, becoming his nineteenth Number One hit. Written by Aaron Barker, after an argument he had just had with his son, "Love Without End, Amen" remains a sentimental Strait classic to this day.

The *Livin' It Up* album contains one pleasing musical performance by George Strait after another. Among the most memorable moments are Clay Blaker's "Lonesome Rodeo Cowboy," and the slow waltz-paced "Drinking Champagne." Bill Mack, a disc jockey and one of George's friends in Dallas, wrote it, and George had listened to the tape while on the road. Most of George's albums came together during these long bus trips.

"I've Come to Expect It from You", written by Dean Dillon and Buddy Cannon, is a medium-paced ballad about being mistreated in a love affair, and it remains a staple of '90s country radio. It also ended up becoming the second Number One single to be pulled from this LP. It ended up sitting on top of the Country Singles chart for five weeks. This was the first time any artist had done that since 1977 when Dolly Parton's "Here You Come Again" blasted her career into the mainstream stratosphere.

On the cover of *Livin' It Up* George is seen wearing one of his black cowboy hats, a black tuxedo jacket, a formal white pleated tux shirt and bow tie, and his blue jeans. Around his waist is a brown leather belt with a huge silver cowboy's belt buckle, on which is emblazoned "CMA Entertainer of the Year."

On his previous dozen albums, only two had featured George with a black cowboy hat; on the others he had worn white. This tipped off a huge controversy in the press. Strait found it amusing how much ink he received over this sudden change in his hat choices. "I've been asked that a million times." He laughed at this obvious tempest in a teapot. "There's really nothing significant about it at all. Really, it's just a personal preference. I still wear white hats sometimes. Then I'll go back to wearing a black one.

I think people get into that good guy/bad guy deal with the black and white hats a little too much. I think that's kinda silly, don't you?"[79] George Strait without his white cowboy hat? It was comparable to Dolly Parton without her big blonde wig or Billie Holiday without her gardenia!

On August 23, 1990, George was the star of his own in-concert television special on The Nashville Network (TNN). Entitled *George Strait Live From Tucson,* the Poteet, Texas, native and his Ace in the Hole band brought their brand of country musical magic into living rooms across America. The television special at the Tucson Convention Center was broadcast live via satellite. The concert was such a huge success that it was rebroadcast on August 27, for everyone who was unable to catch the simulcast version of the program.

On October 8, 1990, the Country Music Association Awards were telecast live from Nashville. Nominated again for Entertainer of the Year was George Strait—alongside Clint Black, Kathy Mattea, Ricky Van Shelton, and Randy Travis. When asked if he'd like to win the award a second year in a row, he replied, "Heck yeah, but that's almost too much to ask."[80]

Calculating the odds of George beating out strongest contender Randy Travis, in USA *Today* writer David Zimmerman was very specific as to where he placed his bets: "Strait's strength is in the fact that he has built perhaps the steadiest career in country music. Ever since his swingy-shuffly music fanned the embers of regional Texas music in the early '80s, his popularity has had no downtime, only ups."[81]

All of this on top of the fact that that year, *People* magazine named him one of their "50 Most Beautiful People." If it were anyone else but George that all of this was happening to, they might start requiring a larger-sized cowboy hat for the cranial increase. Not so Mr. Strait. He remained his cool, confident, and humble self. When October 8 came up, Strait was again CMA's Entertainer of the Year.

There was already talk about George making his movie debut. At the time the film was to be a western of the 1880s ilk and costar Ben Johnson and Karl Malden. This was a project that was to go through several changes and revisions before the cameras ultimately rolled.

The press was already asking him who his favorite films and movie stars were. George reported at the time, "I love Jack Nicholson. He's maybe the greatest actor of the decade. I loved him and Marlon Brando in *Missouri Breaks.* And *The Outlaw Josie Wells,* with Clint Eastwood, is probably my all-time favorite western."[82]

Speaking of his brief performance in the 1982 Ken Wahl film *The Soldier,* George explained, "I was in that one movie with my band. We were in this scene in this club, and a fight breaks out and we're supposed to keep on playing like nothing ever happened. That was pretty natural for us, since that *did* happen a lot back in the honky tonk days! I'm looking forward to trying something like that again. Hopefully, this summer we'll be going overseas to film some westerns. We were going to do it last year, but we didn't get it worked out in time. It would be something new and different, and that's what I like about it. But you never know, it might turn out to be the dumbest thing I ever did in my whole life!"[83] Only time would tell.

When it came to his musical career, now that he was at the top of his musical fame and creative mastery, George Strait was carving out a legendary pedestal all his own. But what was his life like when he was offstage and not in the recording studio, or not accepting one award after another?

He could generally be found on his ranch in Texas. To relax, George counts hunting and rodeo events as among his favorite pastimes. He does a lot of deer hunting. He feels some of the best white-tailed deer hunting in the world is in Texas, though he hasn't gotten any yet. A lot of his relatives go down to visit him. People come and go at the ranch all the time.

As his fame had grown, so had the magnitude and stature of his annual June team roping rodeo. "It's a really neat thing. I'm proud of that. My brother and I put it on. We have a two-headed on Friday, which means you rope two steers on Friday, and then we take the top twenty-five teams back on Saturday and they rope three head. We get trailers and saddles and buckles and lots of prizes. Saturday night I play a dance there. We have a great time. It's a lot of fun. I love to team rope and do it as much as I can. When I can't team rope, I play golf."[84]

In the first eight years of holding this annual event, has George ever won? "No, I never have," he laughs. "I rope in it because it's my roping, but I've never won, and I doubt I ever will, unless I quit singing and just start roping. But then we couldn't have the roping!"[85]

Since his ranch is stashed away out in the middle of nowhere, and George is such a regular guy when he is down there, this can lead to some amusing adventures. One night in the middle of nowhere, Strait found himself stranded. "Boy that was pretty embarrassing," he said. "I was down at my ranch, and something was wrong with my truck. So I have this other old truck down there that I drove back when I was in college. I went to go over to see my dad, and his ranch is about thirty-five or forty miles from where mine is. So I decided I'd drive the old truck. So I'm goin' down this old back road. No houses, barely a little ol' two-lane blacktop road. And all of a sudden, the old truck just quits on me. Well, I could see this guy's house way back off the road. And I figured, well, if it won't start, I guess I'll just walk on up there. But pretty soon, his foreman came by in his truck, and I tell him I can't get mine started. And he said, 'Come on up and use the phone.' So I got in his truck with him and his little boy, and he looks at me and goes . . . 'Aren't you . . . ?' And I go, 'Yeh, yeh . . .' I mean, boy, I was real embarrassed. He kept thankin' me for getting into his truck, and I kept thankin' him for giving me a ride! I could just see it in his face, him wondering, 'What's *he* doin' out here in the middle of the night in that beat-up old truck!?' That's the kind of little situation there that will really humble a person. It's the kind of situation that will really keep your feet on the ground.''[86]

Down at his ranch in Texas, George doesn't have a problem with privacy. Fans don't bother him that much, and the ranch is pretty far out of the way, back in the South Texas brush country, almost a two-and-a-half-hour drive from San Antonio. George spends most of the summer at the ranch when he can. Although he'd like to live there full-time, its remoteness makes it inconvenient for his family, and there are no schools.

George doesn't mind people walking up to him and wanting an autograph. The only time he'd prefer some privacy is while he is out eating somewhere.

George is more apt to encounter enthusiastic fans when he is onstage in concert. He remains one of the most accessible performers in the business and loves to have the fans get up close to the stage and take pictures. He enjoys looking out at the audience and seeing them happy. He plays off the audience's fun. He's even had a couple of stage jumpers. They wrap themselves around him and hold on. George just stands up there and smiles. He ends up with lipstick all over his face some nights from people grabbing him as he walks between the hotel and the bus.

George loves to see his fans live and up close when he performs. "As far as people jumpin' onstage," he says, "I like it that people get that excited by the music. I don't mind. I'm like any other musician, in so far as I feed off that kind of energy. And we've got good security, so the ones that get up onstage don't stay there long! But, you know, if I didn't have fans, what would I have? The day I'll start worrying is the day that *nobody's* out there waiting for us!"[87]

At this point in his career George was very relaxed about his fame and his success. He admits that there was a period where it was all very awkward at the beginning, but as he was about to enter his tenth year as a recording star, he had learned to adapt to the demands and pressures of fame. "I think there was some of that, but I'm over that now. I've been in the business long enough now that I've adjusted to it. But yeah—there was a degree of adjustment, because I don't believe I changed all that much, but all of a sudden people treated me different. Some of them, who I'd known forever—I don't know whether it was jealousy or what— but all of a sudden things were going good for me, and they treated me like I was a bad guy for it. . . . Success is a relative thing, and there are lots of other ways to measure it besides money. And sure—I've been real successful at what I do, and I've made a lot of money in the music business these past few years, but it really hasn't changed me. I just see myself as what I am, a successful country singer—nothing more."[88]

No one could be more surprised at his success. "I kind of slap myself. I guess it really hasn't sunk in yet. I'm still a little bit nervous before a show—it's always a new crowd. You see some of the same faces; but the majority of the crowd is always new, and it's still fun," he says.[89]

He modestly claims, "The hardest part of all this is being treated like a star. I hate that. I really do, and it's sometimes hard for me to deal with it. I love my fans, I really do. But, ya know, it's hard for me to take bein' treated that way."[90]

According to his tour coordinator, Danny O'Brien, who was once part of the Ace in the Hole band, "I think the hardest part of all this for George is not that *he's* any different than he ever was, but that all the rest of us are. After the show, he likes to hang out with the band sometimes, but it's sort of like now everybody tiptoes around him. Even *I* look at him differently than I used to. When I first met him, he was just another hillbilly singer. His first record was out, but it wasn't a hit yet. But now, he's *'George Strait.'* "[91]

In spite of his success and his fame, George remained careful not to make political statements, or to lend his name or his endorsement to any. He kept his thoughts to himself. "I'm not a real big talker, even, you know, when I'm not onstage. My opinions are my opinions. And I don't feel like a good place for them is in some magazine for other people to read," he claims.[92]

With so much success, George began to wonder if the only way from this point was down. He thought about it a lot, hoping it would be five or ten years farther down the road. He knew that the music business was all ups and downs. He knew it would be hard to accept when it happened.

With the smooth and successful pace that his career was continuing to steam along at, George promised everyone that he was far from burned out on his career. In fact, he was just getting started.

Chapter Eight

"Holding His Own"

In March 1991 George Strait released his liveliest, swinging-est, most upbeat, and most varied album to date. Entitled *Chill of an Early Fall* this ten-song powerhouse of an LP showcased the best of his many sides: his way with a sentimental ballad, "If I Know Me" and "The Chill of an Early Fall"; a little lighthearted silliness, "You Know Me Better Than That" and "Her Only Bad Habit Is Me"; a touch of Texas, "Home in San Antone"; a country classic, Hank Williams' "Lovesick Blues"; and some Bob Wills and His Texas Playboys western swing, "Milk Cow Blues." The Ace in the Hole band got three showcases on this Strait classic of an album.

It kicked off with the title cut "The Chill of an Early Fall," an excellent, simple and slow ballad by Green Daniel and Gretchen Peters. George sings the song with a nice resonance, performing the lyrics in a pensive and heartfelt way. About the loneliness of an autumn spent alone, and a love affair lost, this is one of his all-time best ballads.

"I've Convinced Everybody But Me" picks up the pace

considerably, as George swings into this quick-paced country romp about remaining glib in the face of the desertion by a lover. It is followed on the album by Dean Dillon and Pam Belford's beautiful love song "If I Know Me," about devotion in the face of an argument, which was released as a single, becoming his twenty-first Number One hit.

The whimsical "You Know Me Better Than That," which was written by Tony Haselden and Anna Lisa Graham, takes the pace back to the energetic side of things. In the song, George is singing about his current love affair, and addressing it to his ex. The new lover finds George perfect and in love with her cat, but his ex knows the real man. George delivers the amusing song with the right amount of lightheartedness that makes it such a charming romp. The song became Strait Number One hit number twenty-two.

Harlan Howard's charming ballad "Anything You Can Spare" again finds George in a pensive mood. Begging for attention like a hungry cat at the dinner table, George turns it into a lush love song.

The album's sixth, seventh and eighth cuts feature the Ace in the Hole band, swinging with a trio of classics: "Home in San Antone," "Lovesick Blues" and "Milk Cow Blues." "Home in San Antone" is straight from the Bob Wills songbook, and George and the boys are truly in their element with a song that combines their home state with authentic Texas swing.

Hank Williams was the first singer to turn "Lovesick Blues" into a country hit. He released it back in 1949, and it was a Number One hit for sixteen consecutive weeks. Hank's original version featured him yodeling on part of the lyrics. When Patsy Cline cut her peppy version of it in 1960, she gave it a sweeping and soaring ending.

George had always liked the song and knew how hard it was to take a Hank Williams song and release it again as a single. But he wanted to cut it for his own personal satisfaction. The sole complaint he got from the radio stations was that they couldn't play it because he yodeled. George vowed to never yodel again.

George and Ace in the Hole perform Kokomo Arnold's "Milk Cow Blues" perfectly. This was another song that Bob Wills & His Texas Playboys had turned into a classic of the swing genre. This time around it really swings, and it shows off Strait's expressive and jazzlike Texas swing singing. They had been doing the song for years onstage in a much longer version. They recorded it in the studio just the way they performed it onstage. Bowen decided it was too long and he edited it. Fiddle player Gene Elders gets a nice solo in the middle of it, as do Rick McRae and Benny McArthur, the two electric guitar players. It is a shame that it only exists in a truncated version; still it is effective and fun the way it remains.

George sounds wry and dreamy on the self-deprecating shuffle-paced "Her Only Bad Habit Is Me." Written by Harlan Howard and Don Cook, it continues along a slow and swinglike intro, but it is Floyd Domino's nice piano work that stands out on it. The album closes with the beautiful "Is It Already Time," which Aaron Barker wrote. An emotion-filled ballad about love and devotion right up to death's door. George sings this sad song about love at the end with aplomb, and not a drop of maudlin remorse.

It was a perfect showcase album for George, and his fans agreed that it was a true high-water mark for him. Alanna Nash in *Entertainment Weekly* proclaimed, *"Chill of an Early Fall*—the album George Strait was born to make, and the first one to show the thirty-eight-year-old Texan in complete control of his idiom: The record is a sublime refinement of all the ballads, honky-tonk, and hot Texas dance music he's done before. We get to hear all the different facets of his musical personality; he's no longer just the handsome, capable cowboy singer we used to think he was. . . . There's a new confidence to Strait these days—

he no longer sounds so unassuming ... Through hard work, he's made the most of his talents—and become a modern master."[93]

In *Country Music* magazine, writer Bob Allen opined, "There is a deadly efficiency in the way George Strait and his longtime producer Jimmy Bowen have been cranking out best-selling albums of late ... *Chill of an Early Fall* ... is cut of much the same musical cloth as *Livin' It Up,* and features so many of the same session players that a casual listener might conclude it had been pieced together from outtakes from the same sessions ... Strait's going to have to shoot a little higher than this next time around if he intends to stay in the running."[94]

The fans ultimately won out. Not only did *Chill of an Early Fall* sell a million copies, but it became his fifth Platinum album in a row.

Remaining sharp and staying frosty were suddenly concerns for George Strait. For the past several years he had pretty much been "the cock of the walk" in the country music world. He'd had very little competition on the music charts, with the exception of Randy Travis and Ricky Skaggs, and both of their once-hot careers were seriously cooling off. However, there was a whole new breed of "country hunks" in Nashville, and the competition was heating up.

It was in the 1990s that Nashville saw the beginnings of the concept of marketing country music singing males as "country hunks." In exactly the same way that MTV in the 1980s changed the look of rock stars, CMT and TNN in the 1990s made it a necessity for new country music stars to not only sound great—but to look great in their videos as well. In 1991 George had some pretty sharp-looking competition in the "hunk wars" of the '90s. That year he shared the stratosphere of the country Top Ten with the likes of newcomers Garth Brooks, Clint Black, Alan Jackson, Dwight Yoakam, Billy Dean, Joe Diffie, Mark Chesnutt,

Aaron Tippin, and Vince Gill. When Billy Ray Cyrus arrived on the scene in February 1992, the spotlight on hot-looking male country singers really went through the roof.

It was George who was the leader of the pack when it came to wearing a cowboy hat everywhere he went. The press quickly dubbed them "hat acts." Stetsons were de rigeur with Brooks, Black, Jackson, Chesnutt, and Yoakam as well. At the age of thirty-nine, George Strait was already the elder statesman of this new elite country club.

Later that year, when the Academy of Country Music Awards were handed out, newcomer Garth Brooks emerged the winner. When he went up onstage to accept it, Brooks said, looking at George in the audience, "I'm very happy, but I'm a little embarrassed. I just want Mr. Strait to know he's always my male vocalist."[95]

George appreciated being credited as the inspiration for all of these younger men. "It didn't hurt his record sales either. Although he was a little taken by surprise when guys like Alan Jackson began singing his praises, he soon got used to it, and it was business as usual.

Just in time for the 1991 Christmas shopping season came the release of George's fifteenth album, *Ten Strait Hits*. Essentially this constituted his third "Greatest Hits" package, culled from his 1988, 1989 and 1990 studio albums which were all coproduced with Jimmy Bowen. From the *If You Ain't Lovin', You Ain't Livin'* album came the Number One hits "Famous Last Words of a Fool," "Baby Blue" and the silly love song "If You Ain't Lovin' (You Ain't Livin')." From the *Beyond the Blue Neon* came "Overnight Success" and the Number One singles "What's Going On in Your World" and "Ace in the Hole." Gleaned from *Livin' It Up* were "Drinking Champagne" and the chart-topping "Love Without End, Amen" and "I've Come to Expect It from You." Like the previous George Strait Greatest Hits albums, as of summer 1996, it was still in the Top 20 on the *Billboard* Top Country Catalog Albums chart.

In April 1992 George released his sixteenth album, *Holding My Own*. This was a very unique album for several reasons. First, it was to be the last album that he produced with Jimmy Bowen. In 1989 Bowen had left George's record label, MCA Records, and had become the head of the Nashville operations for Capitol Records' country division, Liberty Records. Although they were longtime friends and buddies, the business situation was becoming a strain.

However, they reunited one last time at the end of September through the beginning of October 1991, at Nashville's Emerald recording studio, to record *Holding My Own*, their tenth album together, not including the Greatest Hits albums. Although it had all of the fine elements of George's previous five discs, it was to be known as George's "lost" album, as it eventually became lost in the shuffle between two of the most powerful albums of George's career: *Chill of an Early Fall* and the soundtrack album for George Strait's first movie soundtrack.

The LP kicks off with uncharacteristic rockabilly fury on Marty Stuart and Wayne Perry's "You're Right I'm Wrong." While he chose songs from some of his longtime favorite songwriters, like Dean Dillon ("Holding My Own"), and he mixed in tunes by some of the most respected songwriters in Nashville (Paul Overstreet's "Trains Make Me Lonesome," and Carl Perkins' "Faults and All") the album missed its mark in finding an audience. Word had spread that George had settled on a script for *Pure Country*, his long-talked-about movie debut, and it looked like his fans were waiting for its arrival.

It wasn't that *Holding My Own* was a bad or a lackluster album; it had simply gotten caught in the crossfire of some of the most dynamic country albums of the decade. Garth Brooks' phenomenal thirteen-million-selling *No Fences* and nine-million-selling *Ropin' the Wind*, Billy Ray Cyrus' eight-million-selling *Some Gave All*, and Brooks & Dunn's five-million-selling *Brand New Man* had a lock on the four top positions on *Billboard* magazine's Country Album chart. The highest position that George's *Holding My Own* album achieved was Number Five.

Still, George was proud of the music that the album contained. With regard to the sentimental song "So Much Like My Dad," he explained, "Jimmy Bowen brought me this song out on the golf course. Talk about unusual phrasing and an unusual melody, this song had it. And I knew to be able to sing this song, I was going to have to really, really work hard on it. I loved the song and I wanted to make it really good. I don't usually do this, but I took that song and listened to it over and over and over until it was just there. I had no trouble when I got into the studio to sing it. I loved it. I love to sing it."[96]

"Trains Make Me Lonesome" was another of his favorites from this LP. George felt it should have been a single, but they only released two singles from the album. When the *Pure Country* soundtrack became available, it pretty much wiped out this album. Paul Overstreet had done the demo, and George admits Overstreet may have gotten the feel of the song just a little bit more.

Curtis Wayne's "Wonderland of Love," an up-tempo affair about the miracle of love, was also one of the album's highlights. "Gone as a Girl Can Get" (with the Ace in the Hole band) and "So Much Like My Dad" did well on the country singles chart, but this became the first George Strait album in years that did not produce a single Number One hit. Some changes clearly had to be made. With the big boom in country music fully under way, George seemed to be getting lost in the shuffle.

Although the album was certified Gold for over 500,000 copies sold, unlike the previous four of his new studio albums, it was not to be certified Platinum. Yet in spite of its lukewarm reception at the record stores, the critics all seemed to love it.

In *Country Music* magazine, writer Geoffrey Himes

claimed, "Strait's new album, *Holding My Own,* proves that he's one of the wittiest singers around and one of the most rhythmically imaginative artists in country music ... On the new album, Strait and his band exercise their swing muscles with more assurance than ever, adding the slippery syncopation even to the ballads ... making an album like *Holding My Own* an irresistible pleasure."[97]

In *People* magazine, critic Ralph Novak glowed, "He doesn't have the biggest hat or the most sensitive act, but among today's younger male country singers, Strait may have the mellowest voice and the strongest knack for picking a song ... As usual, Strait sings in the most straightforward style, as befits someone who has inherited Merle Haggard's spot as Nashville's prime exponent of sheer purty singing."[98]

Probably the hardest chore in country music in 1992 was finding a good song. Things had stretched out in the genre so far that it now encompassed a lot of new elements. Mary-Chapin Carpenter's singing was a hybrid of folk/country, Billy Ray Cyrus sang in a pop/rock/country style, and Dwight Yoakam stretched it into pure rockabilly/rock/country.

Hit song foraging was still one of George's strong points, and one that has truly shaped his chart longevity. It's always tough to find good material and the more people performing and recording, the tougher it gets for any one person to find the good songs. George never really thought of himself as a ballad singer, but he wound up making hits of some. He feels ballads are tough to succeed with on the radio and that the ballad has to be awfully strong to make it up the charts.

Strait says, "When it gets close to the time for me to go in the studio, I start getting songs from publishing companies, from all over. Mainly out of Nashville, Tennessee, but some come out of California, or wherever there's a good songwriter with a song. I don't write my own songs.

It's been a long time since I've written anything, and I just got kind of comfortable doing that. I feel like I've been fortunate to find good songs from other writers. It's worked well for me. So before I record, I probably listen to well over five hundred songs. You have to have a feel for it. I know when a song is right for me. It's really a process of elimination. You start going through all these tapes, play 'em again and again, and you keep at it until you got the very best ten or twelve songs that you can find. Even all the way through the recording session itself, I'm still looking for songs. If I find one that's better than the one I brought in the recording studio with me on that particular day, I'll do the new one.[99]

"I've always thought that the melody is really important," he says. "The melody of a song, if it's different, if it catches my ear right away, I feel like that's a real key thing for me; then I'll go back and I'll make sure that the lyrics are good. But I key on that melody."[100]

After George has the ten to twelve songs he really likes and believes in, and has sung them expressively, the next step is to sequence them on the album so that it doesn't end up resembling a big patchwork quilt. However, George says, "I think some of the songs that George Jones always did, he could sing a serious song, a great ballad, and then turn around and sing a real cute, funny song. But as long as it's a good song, who cares?"[101]

It is very important to note that during this period the stakes at a country music concert had grown at an outrageous and unprecedented rate. There were more and more radio stations converting to the "new country" format, which starred the newcomers like Travis Tritt, Hal Ketchum, Tracy Lawrence, Suzy Bogguss, Pam Tillis, and Carlene Carter. Furthermore, several of the new performers turned their shows into complete extravaganzas like the rock & roll shows of the 1970s and 1980s: grand and glitzy and full of bells and whistles, stage fog and eye-popping pyrotechnics.

While George had been releasing his *Chill of an Early Fall* and *Holding My Own* albums, something dramatic happened in the world of country music that changed the way it was looked upon in the entertainment industry. For decades it had been regarded as merely a small segment of the business, catering to a minor part of the record-buying public. In May 1991, all of that changed forever.

Looking at the whole country music craze of the 1990s from the outside, the general record-buying public might think that country just became popular overnight, and it simply started selling more records and creating more stars. However, it wasn't that simple. The music business itself had been underestimating the impact that country music was having. Prior to 1991, *Billboard* magazine, America's music industry bible, had been tallying the top two hundred albums of the week by sales reports gleaned from record stores and airplay statistics from radio stations. However, the universalization of bar coding—the black and white lines and numbers on the back of everything from albums, to books, to breakfast cereal—made it easier to gauge actual sales figures.

In May 1991, *Billboard* standardized its way of producing their charts, using these bar code-generated sales figures, and everyone found out that several country music albums were selling as well as rock & roll albums. The new method, known as SoundScan, changed everything. Thanks to the elimination of human error, country albums were placing much higher on the charts than anyone had realized they were.

That meant that Garth Brooks, Reba McEntire, The Judds, George Strait, Alan Jackson and everyone else in country music was suddenly competing for chart space alongside Nirvana and Bruce Springsteen. This was proof the "baby boomer" generation's disenchantment with grunge rock and rap had led them to embrace country music in a big way. Garth Brooks and all of the hottest new young acts in country were suddenly acknowledged as the biggest new thing on the music scene.

Garth Brooks most conspicuously benefited from this new wave of album sales tallying. However, Alan Jackson and everyone else in 1990s country music ultimately benefited from Brooks' having kicked down the door for the entire genre of country music. Tanya Tucker, Brooks & Dunn, Clint Black, and the whole new wave of country singers also saw the scale of their careers quickly magnified.

Garth's style was important to the whole scene for additional reasons as well, namely redefining the whole country concert scene. Unlike George Strait, Brooks had grown up in a household filled with all kinds of music. He recalls a virtual battle for the airwaves in his house: "My sister is just a huge Aretha [Franklin] fan, an Ella Fitzgerald fan, Stevie Ray Vaughn, Bonnie Raitt. On the other hand, I had a brother who'd try to kill her whenever she turned on the stereo, because he liked stuff more like Tom Rush, Dylan, who my sister just hated."[102]

Garth's first musical influences were anything but country: "I grew up on the late '70s rock groups: Kansas, Boston, Styx, Queen, Kiss. We'd go and watch these shows, and they'd be so damn entertaining. I said, 'Why isn't anybody doing that in country music?' "[103] When Garth Brooks' career began to blossom, he set the new industry standard of turning his country stage shows into the kind of extravaganza-like concert experiences he had witnessed as a kid whenever he had gone to see bands like Kiss and Queen in concert.

Alan Jackson, and all of the stars of '90s country music, owe Garth a debt of gratitude for bringing a new kind of excitement to the whole scene. The young record-buying public, who once equated country music with hard-drinking middle-aged men like Johnny Cash and Waylon

Jennings, suddenly had a young and buff new batch of heroes to look up to. Not only were the new country music stars like Clint Black, Dwight Yoakam, Aaron Tippin, and Vince Gill producing some great new country music, but they were also pretty good to look at as well. For the first time in country music, there was suddenly a sex-appeal quotient factored into the mix.

It is also important to note that at the same time Garth was leading the pack by upping the ante on the male side of country, Reba McEntire was doing the same thing on the female side of Nashville. She is responsible for taking Dolly Parton's whole "Daisy Mae in Hollywood"-style glamour, and making it snap, crackle and pop. All of a sudden a Reba McEntire concert was a Las Vegas revue, with thousands of dollars spent in lights, props, staging effects and costumes. Reba McEntire trail-blazed the way for flashier stage sets for new female stars like Mary-Chapin Carpenter, Lorrie Morgan, and Wynonna Judd.

The sheer magnitude of the numbers was undeniable. For the first time since *Urban Cowboy,* the audience for country music was growing by leaps and bounds. From 1983 to 1992, the viewing audience of TNN (The Nashville Network) grew from 7 million subscribers to 54.5 million. Country line dancing was becoming a new craze from Tucson (The Wild Wild West) to New York City (Denim & Diamonds) and everywhere in-between.

Once Garth Brooks appeared on the cover of *Time* magazine, *Rolling Stone,* and *Forbes,* country music was no longer seen as appealing to a bunch of hicks chewing on a piece of straw. It was red hot and intensifying by the minute.

For George, certain things had been unfolding in a set pattern that he was going to remain unwavering within. One was the way in which he performed onstage. He wasn't about to develop a stand-up comedy act to enliven his concerts. "I'm not a comedian. I can't even tell a good joke. The people come out to hear me sing, so that's what

I go out to do."[104] The same went for the fireworks and the pyrotechnics.

The media was abuzz with this new raft of country music stars that George found himself amid. Reba McEntire or Garth Brooks seemed to be on the cover of either the *Star* or the *National Enquirer* almost weekly. George refused to play into this game, and had no interest in increasing the number of press interviews that he granted yearly. According to him, "You can get overexposed in this business so easily, especially now that there's so many things that you can do that are available to country musicians. I guess you could do something every single day. But I don't do everything that comes along. Who knows? That may be part of why I'm still around now. I get a lot of opportunities to do things, I guess maybe as much as the next guy. But I don't do a lot of them."[105]

However, he did admit that his manager could talk him into things from time to time. If Erv Woolsey thought something was important, George would think twice about it.

At this point in time it was clear that many changes were underfoot for George Strait. Although he wasn't happy about the way in which his *Holding My Own* album ended up buried on the record charts, he had other things on his mind. He was about to launch the most challenging project of his entire career.

Chapter Nine

"Pure Country"

In the spring of 1992 while George's *Holding My Own* album was in the stores, and he was enjoying the summer airplay of hits like "Gone as a Girl Can Get," the machinery was already well under way for his next big career move. He was going to be the first of the new batch of country music stars to make the leap into becoming a movie star. This was not such a stretch of the imagination, since this path had already been successfully paved in the 1970s and 1980s by Kris Kristofferson, Dolly Parton, Willie Nelson, and Kenny Rogers.

The idea of pop and rock singers making the transition from vinyl stardom to celluloid success has long been a Hollywood tradition. Singers as actors dates back five decades when red-hot former big band singer Doris Day made her film debut in *Romance on the High Seas* in 1948. Although now retired from the screen, Doris has made thirty-nine films to date, and at one point she was the Number One box-office draw in the country. In the 1950s Peggy Lee went from jazz singer to movie star in such films as *Pete Kelly's Blues,* and lent her voice to the Disney cartoon *Lady and the Tramp.*

When rock & roll exploded in the late 1950s and throughout the 1960s, several of its biggest stars took their shot at movie immortality, including Roy Orbison *(The Fastest Gun Alive),* Connie Francis *(Where the Boys Are),* Cher *(Chastity),* Petula Clark *(Good-bye Mr. Chips),* and The Beatles *(Hard Day's Night).* The list continued into the 1970s and 1980s with Prince, David Bowie, Madonna, and Mick Jagger all snagging multiple film deals.

However, the grandest music-star-turns-movie-star was Elvis Presley, when he made his debut in *Love Me Tender* in 1956. A run-of-the-mill western starring Richard Egan and Debra Paget, *Love Me Tender* was turned into a huge box-office sensation the second young Elvis hit the screen. The movie, which cost a million dollars to film, recouped its entire budget in the first week of distribution.

Elvis's shrewd personal manager, Colonel Tom Parker, parlayed Presley's sizzling singing career into a multimillion-dollar empire. From 1960 to 1968 Elvis never toured, so that his legion of global fans had to visit their local movie houses if they wanted to see "The King of Rock & Roll" in action. From 1956 to 1969 Elvis starred in thirty-one films encompassing such smashes as *Loving You* (1957), *Jailhouse Rock* (1957), *King Creole* (1958), *Blue Hawaii* (1961), *Fun in Acapulco* (1963), *Viva Las Vegas* (1964), *Clambake* (1967) and *Speedway* (1968). His thirty-second and thirty-third films were the concert flicks *Elvis: That's the Way It Is* (1970) and *Elvis on Tour* (1972).

The Elvis Presley connection was ultimately to become the key in George Strait becoming a movie star. Ten years after the death of Elvis, Colonel Tom Parker came to see George perform at the Las Vegas Hilton, breaking a record previously set by Presley. Parker saw a magical kind of sparkle in Strait's performance, a friendship was forged, and an open dialogue of thoughts and ideas began to flow between Strait, Parker, and Erv Woolsey. It was through Colonel Parker that another former Elvis business associate, movie producer/promoter Jerry Weintraub, also came into the picture. Weintraub had produced one of the most stinging Hollywood looks at the country music world: 1975's highly controversial and explosive *Nashville*.

A fascinating mutual-admiration society began to be established. As Strait explained it, "The Colonel had been coming to see me perform in Vegas every year. He's told me tons of stories. He told me once that Elvis would have liked me."[106]

Parker, who had seen more potential in Elvis than anyone else had in the 1950s, was convinced that Strait—of all the stars in Nashville—had the undefinable "star quality" that could translate to the screen perfectly. According to Parker, "George Strait reminds me of Elvis in a lot of ways. He's quiet, confident and has this special effect on his fans. Even people who aren't especially fond of country music come to see him because he has that magic, that charisma. He even carries himself like 'The King.' "[107]

As George explains the whole connection to the Colonel, "He keeps telling me I'm going to be the next Elvis. I met the Colonel when he came to see me in Las Vegas. He told me I reminded him of Presley. The Colonel kept telling me, 'You have to start doing movies.' I would just say, 'Yeah, yeah,' and then go on to something else. But he pushed the issue by contacting Jerry Weintraub. Jerry came backstage and asked me if I'd be interested in doing a movie. That's how I ended up doing *Pure Country*. Colonel Parker is really the one who made this happen."[108]

Very happy with the way his career was going at the time, George was apprehensive about taking such a huge step. If the film turned out to be a huge bomb, it could ultimately harm his career, or worse yet—alienate his fans. "I didn't want to jump off into something that was going to be a whole new career thing," said George.[109]

With producer Jerry Weintraub eroding his resistance, George and Erv began to take the proposition more and more seriously. Recalls Weintraub, "He said to me, 'What do I have to gain? I sell a lot of albums. I got a great life. I go out and do seventy-five concerts a year, and I sell out most of them. And I don't know how to act. What is this going to do for me?' "[110]

When George would argue, claiming that he knew nothing about acting, Jerry threw it back at George with the logical advice that acting was only reacting. In 1991 the offer of a film advanced from the talking stages to the drawing board. Many ideas were bantered around, including doing a straight western with cowboys and outlaws, so that they could capitalize on George's horseback riding and cowboy hat image. Finally they decided upon a contemporary love story set against the backdrop of show business, musical fame, and its extreme pressures.

Once the ball started rolling, things began to fall into place very quickly. First came the movie script, and the concept of the movie itself, and most importantly, the dynamics of the character that George was to portray. Again, parallels to Elvis Presley abounded. In many ways, *Pure Country* was a 1990s version of the 1957 Presley film *Loving You.*

In *Loving You,* Lizbeth Scott played Glenda, the slightly manipulative career manager of country/rock singer, Deke Rivers, played by Elvis. Singing the songs "Hot Dog," "Mean Woman Blues," "Teddy Bear," and "Lonesome Cowboy," Presley demonstrates the kind of kinetic energy that made him a star. Sharp as a tack, Glenda knows every promotional trick in the book, and step by step she creates an Elvis-like phenomenon out of this fictional performer.

Glenda wants to change his name and give him flashy clothes and lots of stage gimmickry. A pesky reporter

George Strait, one of Country's Living Legends.

George, shown here performing in New Jersey in November 1986, released two albums that year: *#7* and *Merry Christmas Strait To You*.
(Courtesy: John Lee/Star File)

At a Marlboro-sponsored event in New York City in May 1988 to announce George's upcoming tour, members of the press pressured him as to whether or not he was promoting smoking. George denied it—claiming that the only thing he was promoting was good music.   (Courtesy: Chuck Pulin/Star File)

George smiles for the crowd at a 1989 concert in Houston, Texas.
(Courtesy: Marc Morrison/Shooting Star International)

George and K.T. Oslin at
the 24th Annual Country
Music Association Awards
held at the Disney Studios
in 1989.   (Courtesy:
Ralph Dominguez/
Globe Photos, Inc.)

George was finally named
the Country Music
Association's Entertainer of
the Year in 1989 after five
previous nominations.
(Courtesy: Ralph Dominguez/
Globe Photos, Inc.)

Norma, George's wife and high school sweetheart, gives him a kiss on his win at the 25th Annual Academy of Country Music Awards held in Hollywood in 1990.   (*Courtesy: Ralph Dominguez/Globe Photos, Inc.*)

George holds up his award for the cameras at the 18th Annual American Music Awards.   (*Courtesy: Ralph Dominguez/Globe Photos, Inc.*)

George performing in 1993 at Nashville's Grand Ole Opry House for the
27th Annual Country Music Association Awards ceremony.
(Courtesy: John Barrett/Globe Photos, Inc.)

George and Norma pose for the cameras at the Voice of Music Awards in October 1995. (*Courtesy: Ron Davis/Shooting Star International*)

George and The Ace in the Hole Band performing at the 29th Country Music Association Awards ceremony in October 1995.
(*Courtesy: Andrea Renault/Globe Photos, Inc.*)

Even after a hard day on horseback at his Team Roping Classic, George Strait continues to deliver at this June 8, 1996 post-rodeo concert. (*Courtesy: Troy Sniff*)

George on stage and backstage at the Summit in Houston, Texas in June 1996.
(*Courtesy: Marie Dillon*)

Norma usually limits her public appearances to accompanying George to
awards ceremonies.   (*Courtesy: Ralph Dominguez/Globe Photos, Inc.*)

threatens to unravel things by asking too many questions. In time, Deke feels that he is getting lost in the garish outfits and stage tricks, and falls in love with a young singer named Susan (Delves Hart), who loves him just the way he is—successful or not. Deke experiences an emotional tug-of-war between the public image he is creating and the person he is inside.

There are numerous parallels between the film *Loving You* and *Pure Country*, with many of the events and plot developments very tightly tailored toward the real-life George Strait.

This was a big, and risky, step for Strait, and he knew it. "I hope I can pull it off," he said in 1991. "Ninety percent of the time when an actor tries to become a singer or a singer tries to become an actor, it doesn't really work out. But with the right people, I think we can make a quality movie. The biggest fear I have about making one is somebody laughing at me. I don't mind being laughed at, except when I'm trying to do something serious."[111] One of the most crucial aspects of the film was deciding upon a director. He had to have a hit-making track record, and the ability to instill a sense of self-confidence in the first-time actor who was the film's above-the-title star. They chose Chris Cain, who had just completed two highly successful *Young Guns* western films.

While the film was still in preproduction, it was bantered around whether or not George should take a crash course in acting. Ultimately it was decided against, for fear that he would appear like he was trying to act on screen, instead of just exuding his own brand of natural charm. Said George with regard to professional training, "They said maybe I should have lessons, but I didn't want to, and the director didn't want me to, either. So we just jumped right in."[112]

When the announcement was made that he was actually going to do the movie, and that he was already working on the album, George explained, "It's a western type movie. I'm looking forward to it. It's a new experience, but I won't quit singing. Singing got me to the point where I am right now. That's the most important to me."[113] This was to be a career extension, and did not signify abandonment of his passion for singing.

George fastened his seat belt and prepared for his wild ride into the world of movies, which was very different than standing up onstage and delivering a concert performance. He quickly had to adapt to constantly starting and stopping a scene's action to readjust camera angles, and learn to "hit his marks" at the proper focal points whenever he moved.

To ease him into the process, Cain very wisely chose to initially film those sequences in which George's character performed in concert. Filming commenced on May 7, 1992, at the convention center in Las Vegas. To make George more comfortable, members of the George Strait Fan Club were invited to be movie extras in the audience of the convention center.

When George strode out onto the stage to show his public his portrayal of the character Dusty Chandler, they were startled to see a strikingly different version of George Strait: sporting a ponytail and the dark shading of close-cropped beard stubble.

There are several differences in the George Strait-as-Dusty Chandler character in the convention center sequences that open the movie *Pure Country*. First the music—especially the songs "Heartland" and "Overnight Male"—have a hard rock & roll edge to them. In addition to the beard and ponytail, George wears a flashy leather and studs outfit that is far removed from his usual cotton cowboy shirt and jeans look. As Dusty, George moves more onstage than he usually does in concert. Dusty has a cocky sneer you rarely see cross George's face. There are also the glitzy stage lighting effects missing from a usual Strait concert.

George explains, "I've never seen the need for a big show with a lot of effects. There's a point where you can go overboard with the production end. It just doesn't make sense to me. The cost is incredible, especially to put on a show like this guy is doing in the movie. Besides, I wouldn't be comfortable with that. The way I see it, I just try to do as many songs as I can in a concert. That's why I figure people come to see me: they want to hear the songs, the hits."[114]

Filming these sequences George looks like he is enjoying his stint as a famous country singer portraying a famous country/rock star buried alive in special effects. The scenes are visually exciting, and pass like a breeze. No one was worried whether or not George could perform in the concert sequences. The real test came with the hard-core acting. Keeping scripted dialogue fresh and spontaneous is a true challenge.

To round out the cast of characters were fresh newcomer Isabel Glasser, seasoned and sexy Lesley Ann Warren, and veteran western star Rory Calhoun. George immediately found a supportive friend and comrade in his on-screen costar Lesley Ann Warren. "I was nervous as a cat, and so was everybody else," he recalls. "Once I had rehearsed it a couple of times, she got really intense and made it real for me. She told me to relax and try to be real, to listen to what she said, and respond."[115]

George was well aware that he was the true greenhorn in the cast of experienced actors. Rory Calhoun had been a suave leading man back in the 1950s in big music-filled dramas like Susan Hayward's *With a Song in My Heart*. Lesley Ann Warren had become an overnight star as a teenager when she played the title role in a 1960s all-star version of *Cinderella* which featured Ginger Rogers and Walter Pigeon as the king and queen in the fairy story. In such lofty company she couldn't help but become a star. She is also beloved for her portrayal as the blond bimbo gun moll in the movie *Victor Victoria*, in the early 1980s.

George was awkward about being the movie's star, and learning about screen acting as on-the job training. "I was nervous going into it," he admits. "But after the first scene, I kind of calmed down and figured out that it wasn't so hard after all. I think everybody did a great job."[116]

There is no question that George was more than a little bit nervous about delivering his first lines of serious dialogue to the cameras. "I was a little scared. I *thought* I could do it, and I really wanted to try, but you don't really know how it's going to go until you do it. We shot the big concert scenes first, and that went okay. But the first day I had some serious dialogue, I was really nervous. I was doing a scene with Lesley Ann Warren, and I was nervous because I didn't want these people to be sorry that they committed to make this movie with me. I wanted to be good enough to where they were happy they did it," he recalls.[117]

Director Chris Cain had no idea of George's acting capacity. Already an established superstar, there could be no way of predicting if he would be a humble charmer or an egotist amid a star trip. He was pleasantly surprised. "He's been an absolute pleasure to work with," claimed Cain. "He learned very quickly. Acting is a totally new thing for him, but he figured out where the marks are, how to hit 'em and how to find 'em. He learned to tap into an emotional moment. He's a very together man, and he'll be able to go on in this business—there's no question about that."[118]

George was also very grateful to have an understanding and helpful director in Cain. "Well, Chris helps me a lot," he said during the filming. "He wakes me up. I'm pretty laid back most of the time. He seems to be able to get me pumped to do a scene. They've made it easy for me—Chris, Mr. Weintraub, the other actors, the crew."[119]

His on-screen love interest, Isabel Glasser, had nothing but good things to say about him. "He's just such a nice man. He's been so easy to be around as a person. He's really good at responding and working with you in a scene, and he's got this great sense of humor. There's such a natural confidence and charisma about him as a performer, and he has really transferred all that into this medium."[120]

Another of George's costars in the film is actor John Doe, who is the bass player and singer in the classic punk rock band "X." Doe has a charming and warm smile on camera, and in the role of Earl, he shows the kind of caring-friend performance that really works well on camera. They got along well on the set, however coming from opposite ends of the musical spectrum, George and John didn't strike up much of a friendship off camera.

A lot of the elements of the story were very easy for George to plausibly recreate for the cameras. One of these emotional connections between character and actor came in the scene where Dusty gets disoriented about his fame and the unreal lifestyle that being a superstar can bring. "To be totally truthful, I've experienced the kind of [career] burnout this guy has in the movie," says George. "Back seven, eight years ago, when I was working 250 dates a year, you get to the point where you wonder if you can do that another year. It's not an easy thing to deal with. It's pretty serious. Everything starts happening so fast, you feel like you've lost control. That's kind of what this guy is going through. He's unhappy with a lot of different things in his life. But I'm not like the guy in the movie. I've never been to that point where I'd just walk away from it. I've been close to where I thought I might. This guy actually does it."[121]

After George relaxed into the filming process, and felt comfortable with his own delivery of lines of dialogue, he actually enjoyed it all. With the mystery of the unknown behind him, he began to have fun and give a very confident performance.

To really tailor the role to George's strengths and passions, he was also able to work rodeo roping and riding into the script. Identical to real-life Strait, Dusty ropes and rides like a pro when he isn't onstage or in the recording studio. In the film, George insisted that he perform all of his own rodeo stunts. The director and crew were nervous about this. Erv Woolsey and the band had gotten used to George's hobbies. The Hollywood people wanted to use a stunt double, but George felt uncomfortable having someone else ride and rope for him. He eventually convinced them a stunt double was unnecessary. George was most anxious to do his best to give his rodeo-riding on-screen character a sense of dignity, both onstage and in the rodeo arena, and he felt this could best be achieved if he did both.

To get the real look and feel of Texas, the cast and crew did all of the rodeo scenes on location. "We all knew we'd be here during the rainy season," director Cain reported from the set at the time, "but we haven't lost a day of shooting to bad weather, and we've gotten some amazing sunsets and the real feel and scent of Texas you couldn't get without shooting on location."[122]

As this was a musical film, the songs included in the soundtrack and performed on camera were crucial to the production. George had to have some simple country songs to sing for the part of the film where he returns to his hometown. He also had to have songs that were more characteristically "Dusty" songs for the electric country segments. This came at a time when George and his long-time producer, Jimmy Bowen, decided to part company. The man he chose to take over Bowen's production duties was MCA Records famed in-house producer Tony Brown. According to Tony, "Bowen always said that if you're in doubt, if you have an artist that has a good awareness of who they are . . . follow their instincts. Nine times out of ten you'll win."[123] From this point on, Tony has shared the coproducing duties with George on all of his albums, beginning with the soundtrack LP for *Pure Country* Brown was thrilled to have the opportunity to produce MCA's country-star-turned-movie-star.

Picking the right producer for an album is kind of like a creative marriage. Both Brown and Strait found that they instantly meshed on the song choices, and the directions they took in the studio. "That's what's so great about working with Tony Brown, and working with [Jimmy] Bowen was the same way. We never argued over any song. If I don't like it, I'm not going to cut it. That's just the way it is. I'm just not going to do it. So that makes it easy," claims George.[124]

The most daunting and challenging aspect was putting the album together quickly. It was a trial by fire for Tony Brown. He would have preferred six months to prepare for George Strait, but they just had to buckle down and look for songs.

Explaining his choice of songs on the phenomenally successful *Pure Country* soundtrack album, George said, "I'm kind of particular about the songs I'll do. I picked songs for this album like I usually do for my other albums. I just looked for good material. There were a couple of songs they needed for the movie that were different for me. 'Cross My Heart' is a beautiful song, I think. And they wanted something really big for the opening song, and the musical director, Steve Dorff, came up with 'Heartland.' "[125]

The song "Heartland" had originally been called "Pure Country." There were aspects that both Brown and Strait liked, yet there were parts of it that they didn't like. However, different versions of the song kept coming back to them. They would reject the song and writers Steve Dorff and John Bettis would rewrite it again, polishing the lyrics and finally changing the title.

George has said of this, "We needed a really big song to open the movie. We had to change this one quite a bit from what Steve Dorff brought me originally, but even so I still had reservations about it. It's about as rocked up and popped up as you can get and still pass it along to the country market. I had to remember this was not me—George Strait—doing an album. This was for the character in the movie to sing in a situation that wasn't real. Once I got past that, we got it cut. And it's a big, huge production, this song, and the movie made it that way. The guys in the band really love doing it, and I do, too, now. I'm glad we cut it. The director, Chris Cain, had the idea of using a kid's voice, and he said, 'Why don't we use your son?' I said, 'Great,' and of course Bubba wanted to until he got in the studio. He was pretty nervous; but I got in the vocal booth with him, and that's why you can hear him kind of chuckle at times. I was trying to put him at ease, make him lighten up. It was very special for me to do this with him."[126]

In the context of the film, Bubba's version of the song "Heartland" is supposed to sound jagged and innocent, as though the main character of Dusty had been singing it all of his life. The song bleeds directly into George's hard-driving version of it.

"I Cross My Heart" is one of George's favorite songs that he's recorded. He liked it the first time he heard it. Steve Dorff composed the melody, and George's fans agree with him. Many of them began using this song in their weddings, instead of "You're Something Special to Me."

Clay Blaker's "She Lays It All on the Line" gets a full Western swing rendition. George sounds perfectly in his element on this sharp rockabilly number, complete with the Jerry Lee Lewis-style piano work of John Barlow Jarvis.

"Overnight Male," the powerful Southern rocker, is wonderfully upbeat and swinging. Written by Kim Williams,

Ron Harbin and Richard Fagan, the song plays a big part in the plot of the movie, and is an exciting showcase for George.

Glenn Frey of The Eagles and J. D. Souther provided the beautiful contemporary ballad "Last in Love." A pop ballad, it could easily be right out of The Eagles songbook. It hasn't a single country/western touch; it simply lilts along in smooth pop/rock/folk mode.

Country great Mel Tillis and Wayne P. Walker gave George the effective "Thoughts of a Fool." A bit of classic Nashville, Strait turns this into a sentimental country highpoint.

Monty Holmes and Donny Kees' "When Did You Stop Loving Me" is the soundtrack's sweeping steel pedal guitar-laden sentimental ballad. Strait has a nice resonance to his voice on this ode of lost love. The song could have fit a lot of scenes in the movie. Chris Cain and his wife, Sharon, helped George put the album together for the movie. George had the song on the bus and played it for them. Sharon had tears coming down her face as she listened, and George knew it was going to be a good song.

In the very last days before the album had to be completed, Brown was in a pinch. He still had a hole in the soundtrack that it would take just two more songs to fill. "I had those two—'King of Broken Hearts,' and '[Where] The Sidewalk Ends'—on my desk. And, I was waiting to play 'em for George ... I'm a [writer Jim] Lauderdale fanatic. I love his songs, and so I kept going, 'If we don't have anything else, I'm gonna go pitch these. These would be great. I bet George would love these things.' Well, I played 'em for George at the studio, and he went crazy. He said, 'Let's do these today.' And that's what we did ... The morning he heard 'em, he cut 'em that afternoon!" The following day, Tony's A&R person, Renee Bell, informed him that the pair of songs had previously been presented to the movie producers for consideration, and they had passed on them. Recalls Brown, "I said, 'Too late now, they're in the movie.' "[127]

George concurs, "Those were the first Jim Lauderdale songs I recorded, and from then on I've been such a fan. I think 'The King of Broken Hearts' is one of the neatest songs I have ever recorded. Talk about somebody who can write a strange melody. I heard he wrote that about George Jones. 'The king of broken hearts doesn't know he's a king.' Anyway, Tony Brown brought me the Lauderdale songs in the studio when we were still looking for songs. We were really, really rushing this album because we didn't have a lot of time to do it. It's amazing this album came out the way it did, because we put it together faster than any album I have ever put together. I thought it was a great album once we got it done, but I didn't think we would find the material like we did. Tony Brown brought these in—they were on the same tape—and we got through 'King' and needed another song. I went back and listened to 'Where the Sidewalk Ends,' and said, 'Let's do both of them!' "[128]

When the film finally wrapped up, everyone involved in it was thrilled by the product, and hopeful about its reception. Speaking about the film, producer Jerry Weintraub explained, "This is a story about a country singer and a story about a man in turmoil. It's a family movie and a terrific love story. I think country music fans, who are legion now, will love it."[129]

Weintraub was also very confident that this film was going to be the start of a brilliant acting career for Strait. He felt it was important that George portray a singer in his first movie, and that he continue to sing in his future pictures. "But I think there will come a time when he makes a movie where he doesn't sing. He reminds me of Alan Ladd, back when Ladd was a Number One box-office star. The women are going to go nuts over this guy; the guys like him because he's a man's man. I mean, he did all his own rodeo stuff in this movie. He got on a horse, he's a great rider and he did his own ropin'. He shows up on time. He works real hard. And he's a great guy on top of everything else. I've enjoyed this experience with him more than anything else I've done in years."[130]

George was pretty optimistic about the job he had done on camera, seeing it as a good change of pace. He was also grateful that Jerry Weintraub had given him the chance to do the kind of custom-created movie he could be proud of. "He gave me a great opportunity to do something I wanted to do. I've done it!" he said triumphantly. "It was a lot of work—that was kind of tough. But it was a lot of fun, too. It was a real change for me at that time. All I'd done was concerts and records. To jump into something like making a movie was scary. There was a lot on the line. I could have been just the worst. It might have ended my career. Who knows? But I was real proud of it after I was done."[131]

In his best country "aw shucks it was nothing" tone, George admitted, "I enjoyed it and I did better than I thought I would. If you can get onstage and get a feeling from the crowd, you can get a similar feeling making a movie. It's just another part of the entertainment business."[132]

When the film opened on October 23, it hit Number Six in *Variety*'s Top Box-office chart. The film received generally favorable reviews, with everyone unanimously agreeing that the film was every George Strait devotee's dream. *People* magazine's Ralph Novak had fun flinging mud at it by stating, "If it were any cornier or mushier, it would be chowder, but this vehicle for country singer Strait generates a charming sweetness, the music is lively, and both Strait and Glasser are ingratiating new faces . . . Warren, characteristically actressy, plays Strait's manager . . . This is a cowboy movie where the good guy, when he finally confronts his main foe, doesn't sock the villain or call him out for a gunfight; he threatens to sue him. Somewhere, John Wayne must be curling his lip."[133]

Master critic Roger Ebert, in his syndicated movie review, claimed, "*Pure Country* tells a laborious but likable story, not terribly original, about a country music superstar who tires of performing in big stadium extravaganzas, and begins to yearn for the days when it was just him and his acoustic guitar ... Strait is genuine and has a winning smile, and holds his own in a screenplay that makes few demands ... Dramatic scenes are interrupted by a great many country songs, and everything leads up to a big romantic climax. *Pure Country* is the very definition of the kind of movie where fans of the star will enjoy it more than dispassionate observers. If you like George Strait, you'll see a lot of him here."[134]

While Bob Allen in *Country Music* magazine hated the song "Heartland," he loved the rest of the album. He claimed, " 'Heartland,' the song that opens *Pure Country*, and which, I take it, is the movie's theme song, is a major part of the problem here. It's not only terribly out of sync with the rest of the album; it sounds like a cereal commercial—like an awkward parody of Hollywood's notion of what a country song should be ... Now let's talk about what's good about *Pure Country*, which is naturally quite a lot. For starters, Strait and Brown have seen fit to include two fine, later-day, honky-tonk ballads by Jim Lauderdale: 'The King of Broken Hearts' and 'Where the Sidewalk Ends.' Strait does an exquisite job with them ... he provides just the right gusto on a pair of good-natured, tongue-in-cheek, macho man celebrations: 'She Lays It on the Line' (Clay Blaker) and 'Overnight Male' (Kim Williams/Ron Harbin/Richard Fagan). On 'Last in Love' (J. D. Souther/Glenn Frey), Strait once again reminds us just how much his enduring appeal lies in his strength as a romantic balladeer."[135]

The film begins with a photo montage of old snapshots

of George's character Dusty, tracing his life to adulthood, and his position as the leader of his own country band. While the photos flash up on the screen, the title credit version of the song "Heartland" plays. The innocent and childlike voice from the past is provided by George "Bubba" Strait, Jr. As the credits roll, and the photos continue, mid-song George Strait, Sr., takes over the lead vocals as the photos progress into the snapshots of adult years gone by.

The most important aspect of this photo montage is to show documentation of the friendship of the three central characters in the film played by George Strait, Lesley Ann Warren and John Doe. They are shown in the beginning of a singing career, performing in a honky-tonk, and passing the hat to earn a couple of bucks. As the last credit rolls, the camera zooms in to show the front of a dollar bill being tossed into the hat—signifying that money now somehow plays a key role in the action.

The action begins in a crowded auditorium, with the sold-out audience chanting the name "Dusty" in anticipation of the show about to begin. As the house lights dim, the crowd cheers wildly, pyrotechnics explode onstage, and from the glare of the fireworks, from amid the smoke, emerges the unmistakeable silhouette of George Strait. As Dusty, he sports Don Johnson/*Miami Vice* beard stubble on his face, wears a flashy cut jacket, and his ponytail wags below the brim of his cowboy hat. He surveys the cheering crowd, and proceeds to swing into a hard rocking version of "Heartland." It is a song unlike anything that Strait has ever done. It is countryfied—but it is one hundred percent rock & roll.

The number is a visual treat. It is as if Garth Brooks had designed a flashy stage show for George—but it is clearly not the kind of show he would ever give. Then he and his band swing into their second number, "Baby Your Baby," a rhythmically rocking ballad.

While it plays, his manager, Lula (Lesley Ann Warren), is introduced in the sidelines. She is the 1990s version of the manager Lisbeth Scott played in Elvis' *Loving You.* However, instead of Scott's smart cotton shirtwaist dresses, Warren wears form-fitting, brightly colored leather dresses and skirts. Lula is having a romantic fling with Buddy (Kyle Chandler), a cute, hunky member of Dusty's road crew. Clearly, Buddy longs to one day be in Dusty's shoes and is on a mission to weasel his way onto the path to fame himself. He has written a song that he wants Dusty to record. Using his affair with Lula as his entree to song-writing, Buddy provides the catchy upbeat tune "Over-night Male."

Dusty is clearly getting burned out on his special-effect-laden show. The next night, onstage, he omits part of one of his big songs, and the crowd is totally unfazed by his temporary lapse. It is a moment of clarity for him, as he discovers that he is being merely used as a focal point for all the lights and pyrotechnics, and that his music has become replaceable and irrelevant. It is lost in all of the glitz and smoke, and with it he has lost his drive and his focus.

On a lark he runs away, and returns to the rural Texas home of his Grandma Ivy (Molly McClure) to look for his roots. He gets drunk at a local honky-tonk, and gets into a fistfight defending the honor of Harley Tucker, played by Isabel Glasser. She lives on a ranch with her father, Ernest (Rory Calhoun), and her two brothers J. W. (Toby Metcalf) and Tim (James Terry McIlvain). Their once-grand ranch is down to its last thousand acres, and the family is staking their performance at an upcoming rodeo in Las Vegas as their last hope to save it. Hungover Dusty decides to help them achieve their dream.

While Dusty is getting back to basics, he misses a major concert date. Unwilling to give back the box-office money, Lula decides to intensify the stage smoke and lighting, and sends Buddy out onstage to lip-sync the part of Dusty. It works and no one in the crowd is the wiser.

The plot thickens when Buddy threatens to blackmail Lula. Dusty's drummer, Earl (John Doe), tracks down Dusty. The controversy over Buddy's performance explodes in the news when he sells the story to the tabloids. Harley has fallen head over heels in love with the nonfamous Dusty she thinks she knows, until Lula shows up, claiming to be his wife. Harley dumps him like a hot potato, and everything seems to be in shambles.

However, by the end of the film, blackmailing Buddy gets what he deserves, Lula gets Dusty back to tour in his new back-to-basics show, Harley learns Dusty's real identity as a star, and the pair fall madly in love. To wrap up the story even neater, Ernest and Grandma Ivy hook up as elderly lovebirds. It is really quite a charming story, told to a lot of great new George Strait music.

George's importance in the show business realm was simply magnified from that point on. The *Pure Country* soundtrack album not only hit Number One for several weeks, but it has gone on to become the most successful album of George Strait's career. Having sold over five million copies, it was still on the *Billboard* Country Albums sales charts and in the Top Forty three years later.

Having successfully made the quantum leap from singing star to movie star, George Strait wasn't ready to rest upon his laurels. "I hear this a lot," he says. " 'Well, you've accomplished all you can accomplish in country music.' I don't feel that way. I'm not through, and I think I've got a lot more to go."[136]

Chapter Ten

"Strait Out of the Box"

The dust had barely settled from George's triumphant
romp on the silver screen in *Pure Country* and it was already
time to return to the recording studio. There was no question that the film and the soundtrack album were roaring
successes, so Strait and his new producer, Tony Brown,
had to come up with a red-hot follow-up LP.

Not only was George proud of the job he had done in
his acting debut, but Erv Woolsey was also as happy as a
clam in mud. The movie had given his career a boost as
well.

In April 1993 George and Tony Brown convened at
Sound Stage Studios in Nashville and cut his million-selling
eighteenth album, *Easy Come, Easy Go*. When it came to
selecting songs for this album, George found himself rely-
ing on several of the same writers who had made the *Pure
Country* album such a huge hit, including Steve Dorff, Clay
Blaker, and Jim Lauderdale, plus his favorite, Dean Dillon.

The first time he heard the demo for Dean Dillon and
Aaron Barker's "Easy Come, Easy Go" he flipped over it.

The only problem was that he had to wrench it away from Dean Dillon first. Dillon had another record deal at this time, and they wanted this song to be his first single. George convinced Dean to give it to him. The song went on to become George's twenty-fifth Number One single. The South-of-the-Border/Calypso sound of the song was a perfect radio hit. With George's lush voice bidding his lover "goodbye," "farewell" and "vaya con digs," it was a huge smash for him on the charts, and became a "radio active" single, receiving plenty of airplay long after it had fallen off the charts.

The beautiful, mournful ballad of devotion, "The Man in Love with You," really showed off the romantic side of George's expressive singing style. It was another Steve Dorff love song with the kind of pretty melody George did well with. Although some of the critics don't like these tunes, the buying public does, and that matters most. George's fans loved this one, and it immediately became George's twenty-sixth Number One single.

In the context of the song, George is heard apologizing for his faults, but confessing his undying love as the one perfect thing about him. It was really tailor-made for him, in that he sings about not always being the hero in the "white hat." Well, just to cover both sides of the coin, the album package showed Strait in both his trademark white hat and his black hat.

When he was asked at the time about his track record, George replied, "Wow, that would be great to have twenty-six more. I think that would be a little greedy, though, don't you?"[137] Greedy or not, at last count he had added nearly ten more Number Ones to the list.

In the tradition of George adding some older classic country cuts to his albums, on this album he dug into the George Jones songbook for the silly love song, "Lovebug." Lyrically, the song is about as serious as "Itsy Bitsy Teenie Weenie Yellow Polkadot Bikini" (Brian Hyland, 1960).

Strait knew it was silly when he cut it, but he felt that he needed it to lighten up the tone of the album. According to him, "I think George Jones, who had some great serious ballads, also cut some really neat, funny songs. And I like those kinds of songs. What's neat about this is that Curtis Wayne, who writes for us now, wrote 'Lovebug.' And of course I knew the song but never thought about cutting it until Curtis pitched it to me. It's hard for me to even think about doing a George Jones song. Of course, George's version is better, but I think mine is different."[138]

Jim Lauderdale was becoming one of his new favorite writers, and on the *Easy Come, Easy Go* album, George cut two of his songs. He really appreciated Lauderdale's way of lyrical phrasing. Lauderdale had the tendency to construct phrases in different ways, and he came up with unique melodies. George chose the album opener, "Stay Out of My Arms," a fast-paced country dance number that kicked off the LP with the right amount of snap, crackle and pop. He also recorded Jim's witty up-tempo ditty, "I Wasn't Fooling Around."

After working together a couple of times now, George and Tony Brown were perfectly meshing as coproducers. Tony was amazed and amused about the speed with which George Strait recorded his albums. He had the habit of knocking out a whole ten-cut album in two weeks' time— give or take a day or two. Tony claimed George worked so fast because he wanted to get back to Texas.

The *Easy Come, Easy Go* album hit the stores in September 1993, and sailed into the Top Ten. It ended up peaking at Number Two on *Billboard* magazine's Country Album chart. It didn't capture Number One because the multimillion-selling *Common Thread: Songs of the Eagles* album was locked in at the top of the charts for several weeks.

On Labor Day 1993, George and several of his country buddies headlined the Alamo Dome in San Antonio. As Danny O'Brien, vice president of the Erv Woolsey Agency and George's tour coordinator, explained, "It's something we wanted to do, a big event for the city he lives in. After looking at it, we got together with PACE Concerts and decided to do a big special event. What a wonderful way to bring people to the city and have a good concert and let people experience Texas hospitality. George has a huge national fan club. I'm sure a lot of fans will come from all over the country."[139] Also on the bill that hot Texas day were Suzy Bogguss, Lee Roy Parnell, and Brooks & Dunn.

In 1993, big all-star tribute albums were quite the rage, including the aforementioned *Common Thread,* which featured Alan Jackson, Tanya Tucker, Lorrie Morgan, and John Anderson. Usually, George passed on these big benefit-fueled albums. However, one all-star package came his way that he couldn't resist. It was Asleep at the Wheel's Grammy Award-winning *Tribute to the Music of Bob Wills & His Texas Playboys.* Ray Benson, the leader of Asleep at the Wheel, assembled an all-star cast to end them all: George Strait, Dolly Parton, Chet Atkins, Vince Gill, Marty Stuart, Lyle Lovett, Suzy Bogguss, Huey Lewis, Willie Nelson, Merle Haggard, Brooks & Dunn, and Riders in the Sky.

On the album, George Strait and Ray Benson are heard duetting on the festive dance reel, "Big Ball's in Cowtown." On the cut, Strait is clearly in Western swing heaven. Explains George, "I've done this in my show for a long, long time. It's a great old Bob Wills tune. When Asleep at the Wheel was doing that Bob Wills tribute album, they asked me to do it, and I was glad to be able to. Asleep at the Wheel is a great group, and I know most of the guys in the band personally. I admire what they have done and have a lot of respect for the kind of music they do. Years ago, we opened up for them at Gruene Hall. That's the place where Ray Benson is right in his element. He is such a great guy, a great performer, entertainer, producer, and has a band that can swing as good or better than anybody, and I was glad to do this song with them."[140] Recording the song was also very convenient for George, as it was cut at Bismeaux Studios in Austin, Texas. If this cut has a Texas feel to it, it is fittingly so!

In April 1994 George and Tony Brown came together at Nashville's Emerald Studios to record his next album, *Lead On*. In addition to his steady stable of writers he draws upon—including Jim Lauderdale, Dean Dillon, Sanger D. Shafer, and Aaron Barker—George began to tap some different writers. On the new list came Bob McDill (who wrote Alan Jackson's brilliant "Gone Country,") and Max D. Barnes.

The album began with the sensitive, contemporary ballad "You Can't Make a Heart Love Somebody." George turns on the expressive waterworks in this song about a woman turning down a man's wedding proposal. Slow, sad, and brilliant, it shows George off at his best. Jumping off to New Orleans for the cajun-flavored "Adalida," George snaps freshly to form on this exciting and unique number. With fiddles wailing, and lyrics about "Etroufee" and swimming in the Pontchartrain, this is the most exciting cajun romp to hit a record since Mary-Chapin Carpenter's "Down at the Twist and Shout."

On Wayland Holyfield and Bob McDill's "I Met a Friend of Yours Today," George has the blues. Reviving Mel Street's 1976 hit, Strait really delivers the goods on this story song about realizing his wife is having an affair.

He really croons on Jim Lauderdale and Terry A. McBride's "Nobody Has to Get Hurt," a mid-tempo song about learning from love's mistakes. On Dean Dillon and Teddy Gentry's title cut, "Lead On" George takes it slow and sensitive. A ballad about a budding love affair, George sounds great with Liana Manis singing the harmony vocal behind him.

Another highlight on this album is Gerry House and Devon O'Day's "The Big One." George amusingly explains the evolution of this cut by saying, "I like this record a lot; I just wish I hadn't done that real high part in the song because it's real hard to do. Sometimes I end up sounding like Tarzan when I do it live. On the demo, the song stops real quick, just cuts off. And then they had a big rumbling, like an earthquake. So we did that at first on ours. Then I started thinking about 'Marine Del Rey' and the birds at the end. So I told Tony Brown to get the rumble out of there. He agreed and we took it out."[141]

When this album was released in November 1994, it went right up to the top of the charts to settle in at Number One. It was certified Platinum for a million copies sold, and brilliantly continued the George Strait musical legacy. In *CountryBeat* magazine, critic Craig Peters proclaimed, "You can always count on George for ten satisfying slices of pure country, and with *Lend On,* he once again delivers the goods . . . George has been taking criticism from some quarters for having found a formula and sticking to it: a couple of shuffles, a couple of heartbreakers, a couple of foot-stompers, and—BAM!—a few more hits and another Gold (or Platinum) record. But is that such a bad formula, after all? . . . In the wide sweep of George Strait's career, *Lead On* is hardly a landmark release. But it is head and shoulders above ninety percent of the new product that's out there—and one more addition to the formidable recorded legacy that may ultimately threaten to match that of the other George before it's all over."[142]

In 1995 it came time to take a long look back at George's brilliant career. He had released nineteen albums, had hit the Number One slot in *Billboard* magazine thirty times, had become a movie star, and was looked at as the absolute king of traditional country music. To celebrate all of his accomplishments, it was decided that the time had come for a four-CD boxed set retrospective of the best of George's classic music, plus some previously unheard gems from his past, a new cut or two.

The result was the brilliant *Strait Out of the Box,* featuring seventy-two of George's best and brightest performances. When he was asked why he was releasing this boxed set at this time, he replied, "Mainly, [because] MCA [Records] was ready to do it. It didn't take much arm twisting for me. I really wasn't obligated to do it, not at all. I just think it was a neat thing. You see a lot of box sets, and usually the people you see them on aren't here anymore. So I was happy to be able to do one now while things are still going great for me."[143]

George had been so busy living in the present that it was a pleasure to take a look back at the many paths his career had taken. "You know, you tend to forget about things as years go by," he says. "When I started looking back and thinking about all these songs and things we did, like on those D Records we did back in Texas, it brought back a lot of memories that just kind of slipped your mind through the years. Going down to town in a pickup truck with equipment loaded in the back. Setting up and tearing down every night, and all the things that happened along the way. You go back and you start remembering what led up to this song, why you picked it, where you heard it. It was fun to remember all that. I enjoyed making it. I gotta be pushed into a lot of things, but I was glad about this one."[144]

Strait Out of the Box was released in September 1995, and has gone on to become one of the biggest-selling boxed sets of compact discs ever released, with over three million copies sold. Not Barbra Streisand, not Crosby, Stills & Nash, and not Fleetwood Mac—but GEORGE STRAIT. And, a full year after its release, it was still on *Billboard* magazine's Top Country Albums chart.

The first of four disks begins with three of George's eight cuts for D Records in Texas, including "I Just Can't Go On Dying Like This," "(That Don't Change) The Way I Feel about You," and "I Don't Want to Talk It Over Anymore." Reminiscing, George claims, "This album reminds me of a lot of great times I've had from the very first song . . . back in the old days of hauling our equipment around in the back of pickup trucks . . . It was real interesting to remember all of those things, and then when we finally got the thing finished, to have it all put together in one set of everything I've done—even songs that people never really got to hear except for me and a producer. We were just a local band that never got much publicity. I mean, why should it have? We were just plugging around in the bars and honky-tonks.''[145]

The previously unreleased songs included "What Would Your Memories Do" from the aborted Blake Mevis album, and "I Thought I Heard You Calling My Name" which was cut from his fourth album. George, who personally selected all of the cuts to be included on this boxed set, was mindful to include four cuts from his pre-*Pure Country* disc. The *Holding My Own* album had only been just released when the movie deal came along. The *Pure Country* soundtrack pushed the earlier album aside. A lot of songs were never released.

When performers put together a career retrospective album, it often suggests the end of an era for them. According to George, *Strait Out of the Box* didn't signify the beginning or ending of anything; it was a juncture, not a departure.

While surveying this wealth of material, George was reminded of several of his favorite songs that he had long ago stopped performing in concert. "I was doing the Labor Day show we do in San Antonio," he says, "and the radio station there played everything I've recorded in one day. I was playing golf and listening to the radio, listening to all this, and I heard songs I had totally forgotten about. I really enjoyed that. Some of the songs I cut I'm really proud of. I didn't write them; I just cut them. I still think they were great songs. I started thinking, 'Man, I need to do that song again in my show!' I'm going to try and do that, to work some of them in. I used to do a lot of them. As time goes on, you drop one here, and you drop one there. You do new stuff.' "[146]

Strait says, "I went into the studio and recorded two new songs for the set. Probably both new songs will be released as singles."[147] From this session came two consecutive Number One singles: "Check Yes or No" and "I Know She Still Loves Me."

"Check Yes or No" was the first song to be released as a single. According to George, "The whole idea of this song is like when you are in the third grade and you write the girl you like a note that says, 'Do you like me? Check "yes" or "no." '; I remember coming back from Nashville after cutting this, and I was taking Bubba to school. He's usually in a bad mood in the morning and he doesn't talk much. I said, 'Bubba, I'm gonna play you this song, and I know you're gonna love it.' I could tell he was really perking up. He finally smiled and said, 'I was trying hard not to like it, but it's a cool song.' "[148]

He followed it up with "I Know She Still Loves Me," a good ballad that a lot of people could relate to.

Probably the most unique song on the boxed set is the previously released "Fly Me to the Moon," a duet between George Strait and his life-long idol Frank Sinatra. In 1993 and 1994, Frank Sinatra released two Top Ten albums of duets with some of the hottest stars of the 1990s. The first one, *Duets,* included Sinatra teamed with Barbra Streisand, Aretha Franklin, Carly Simon, Anita Baker, Bono, Luther Vandross, Liza Minnelli, and Gloria Estefan. *Duets II* released a year later, included Linda Ronstadt, Patti La-Belle, and Lorrie Morgan.

Approaching his eightieth birthday, Sinatra was too busy to deal with all of these singers' schedules, so he went into the studio with Phil Ramone and recorded his vocals, and then all of the other stars recorded their vocals as time permitted. Each of the cuts was pieced together in the studio and then released. Both albums were enormously successful, award-winning million-sellers.

Apparently, more cuts were recorded than were used, and the duet between George Strait and Frank Sinatra was one that was left "in the can" for two years. According to George's writer buddy, Frank Dycus, "Most people don't know it, but George Strait is a Frank Sinatra fan. He loves that kind of music—'One for My Baby (One More for the Road),' 'Learnin' the Blues'—they're pop but they're still kind of a barroom, urban honky-tonk."

Says Strait, "I've always been a fan of Frank Sinatra, and I've listened to his music for a long, long time. You just can't beat the big band swing. He's such a great singer. I met him one time in Texas, went to his show and went backstage right before he was getting on. He's a classy guy." George laughs. "I was kind of let down [because Sinatra didn't use the song] because I thought it turned out really good. I was really mad. I really liked the cut that we did!"[149]

Explaining the evolution of this song, which was recorded in October 1993, George says, "Tony Brown asked me if I was interested in doing a duet with Frank Sinatra for a record he was doing, an album with some country on it. And of course, I've been a Sinatra fan for years and I've always said that. I think Frank Sinatra is a great singer and I love great singers; I don't care what kind of music they sing. He does that big band stuff and I love that music. I'd love to cut an album someday and do that kind of music. And so when I had the opportunity to do it, I said, 'Hell yes!' So there was a list of songs to choose from, and I picked 'Fly Me to the Moon' from what was left. If I had my choice, I would have picked 'Luck Be a Lady Tonight.' But anyway, Frank did his part, then me and Phil Ramone, the producer, went in the studio and I did mine. I thought it turned out great, and I'm sorry he didn't use it on the album. But I'm proud of it and glad people can hear it now."[150]

There were so many consistencies in all of George's previous nineteen albums—a little swing, a couple sad ballads, an up-tempo number or two, and exactly ten cuts per album (with the exception of two versions of "Heartland" on the *Pure Country* soundtrack)—George has sometimes been accused that all of his LPs are repetitious. He doesn't feel that way. He chooses the songs he loves and feels all of his albums are different.

He now had three consecutive full albums of material recorded with Tony Brown producing. George was extremely happy with their relationship, both professional and personal. He liked Tony as a friend and respected him as a producer and as a musician.

If one had to discuss the two passions of George Strait, one of them would be singing and the other one would definitely have to be riding on the rodeo circuit. George's huge success over the last fifteen years has enabled him to pour money into his annual team roping rodeo event every June on his Texas ranch. When asked if there would ever be a day when he would give up singing and concentrate on roping he says, "I've dreamed a long time about turning pro. Outside of my wife Norma and my son Bubba, rodeo is my true love. I'd do most anything to be a permanent part of it."[151]

He says with no small degree of Texas pride, "Our team roping event is probably one of the best in the country. We get the best ropers, including many professional ropers who compete in the National Finals in Las Vegas. I'd really like to have more time to concentrate on my team roping, but I doubt I'll ever get to the point where I can compete professionally. Still, that's been a dream of mine for a long, long time."[152]

He loves the sun, the soil, and his livestock: "I keep an eye on the cows, but I love messing with my horses the most. . . . I've got some really good horses and an opportunity to do it [compete professionally]. That's been a dream of mine for a long, long time."[153]

When he isn't roping a steer or riding a horse, George enjoys playing golf and doing the things he doesn't get a chance to do when he's on the road. During the summer at the ranch he can relax and not think about anything else except his cows, his horses, and roping. It takes his mind off the road.

One of the biggest criticisms that Strait receives regards his deep sense of privacy. Whenever Dolly Parton has a new facial nip or tuck, it is on the cover of the *National Enquirer* or the *Star*. As public as so many stars' lives are, that's just how totally private Strait's life remains. According to Erv Woolsey, "George is one of these guys, he's always happy to talk about the music, the records. He's a private person. I've heard him called everything from 'shy'—he's not shy. He'll sit there and tell you exactly what he thinks."[154]

Says George, "I decided a long time ago that I needed some time to myself. I didn't mind talking about the music and the music career, but my personal life is just that. Personal! And that's the way I like to keep it. I've never really been treated unfairly by the media. I have no horror stories to tell. Maybe that's because of me or maybe it's not. I mean, I'm sure it upsets some people at times. I just made up my mind, as I say, a very long time ago that that's the way I was going to do things. I remember thinking, 'If it works, fine, and if it doesn't, I'll only have myself to blame for it.' Fortunately, for me, it's worked out all right."[155]

Chapter Eleven

"Nashville Takes a Strait Look at George"

One of the most important perspectives on George Strait had to come directly from the city where the core business of country music all takes place: Nashville, Tennessee. The ideal source had to be directly connected to the inside circle of Music City, had to be close enough to know George Strait, and to have observed all of the inner workings and professional decision making that went on in his career. Yet, he also had to be someone who was far enough removed from George's career so that he could remain objective and candid.

I found such an ideal source in record producer Mick Lloyd. I had spoken to him a couple of years ago about another country singer he was managing at the time. Mick's observations are frank, unbiased, and fascinating:

BEGO: I wanted to talk to a Nashville insider about what the music business was like when George Strait first came to town, and the kind of impact that he has had on the country scene. First of all, I wanted to ask you about some of your experiences, which make you an expert in country music, as I know that you have met George several times, and have followed his career.

LLOYD: Well, I came here as an artist in 1976. I was on three different labels. I came here and I signed with GRT Records, which at the time had Johnny Lee, Earl Thomas Conley, Alabama. It was a really significant label. That was my last label, and after that I went into producing and publishing. Since that time I have produced people like Johnny Lee; Slim Whitman; John McNally, a big international star; The Star Sisters, who went Platinum in Europe; a group called Ride the River, on Polygram, which has done real well, so I currently produce six or seven acts. My publishing companies have done quite well, I have several Gold and Platinum hits, and I own an interest in a studio. I have also won a lot of songwriting awards.

BEGO: Give me one of the song titles that George's fans might be familiar with.

LLOYD: Slim Whitman's "Precious Memories" and "Beyond the Sunset." John McNally's "Sometimes When We Touch." I was also one of the leading people in the country dance explosion. I was responsible for the music on a series of dance instruction videos, which sold three million copies.

BEGO: Everyone talks about George Strait being the first person to bring back new traditionalism in the current country music scene. If he brought it back into fashion, what was the country music scene like in the late 1970s and early 1980s, when George Strait was first knocking on doors in Nashville? Before the movie and soundtrack album for *Urban Cowboy* exploded on the charts, what was the atmosphere in Nashville like? Was it still just Willie Nelson and The Highwayman who were making waves?

LLOYD: Well, in the late '70s, a *very* small segment of the market was country. The *Urban Cowboy* album is what really brought it into the mainstream, and George Strait actually followed that. He came along right after the *Urban Cowboy* thing, and in many ways, he was the one who was the antithesis of the *Urban Cowboy* movement. I guess that you could say that he was really the first hat act . . . But, what is amazing to me, about him, more than anything else, is that his first big hit was in 1981 . . .

BEGO: "Unwound" . . .

LLOYD: Exactly. And, his longevity is absolutely unbelievable. Because, he is the only guy who is still being played consistently—in any sense of the word—who goes that far back.

BEGO: Yes, and it is Randy Travis who would directly follow George, longevity wise.

LLOYD: But Travis' first hit was in 1985, so really there would be a four-year difference between the two. Because when I looked it up the other day—because I was really kind of curious myself— as to when George's first hit was, and it was in 1981. It is really amazing that he is as popular today, because no one who is popular today dates back to 1981. Most people don't realize that he has been around that long.

BEGO: You're right, especially the young kids who are buying his records today. . . . What do you think that the reason is for his longevity?

LLOYD: I think that it is the fact that he is really a nice guy; everybody has always liked him; he hasn't made any enemies. He is a good family guy, never was a publicity hound, *and* he has always cut good songs. That is probably the biggest thing. He has always cut good, good songs. There never was a controversy about him, and virtually everything he has done has gone Number One. It's an unbelievable run.

BEGO: Right up to today, in 1996.

LLOYD: Right. It's incredible. He's one of the first guys who really started recording with his own [touring] band, and has done that to this band.

BEGO: I know that he only has them on a couple of cuts per album, and he often uses studio musicians.

LLOYD: Right, but I know he was one of the first guys [in Nashville] who ever took his [touring] band and put them in the studio—at all.

BEGO: Now, what would be the logic for not using them all of the time in the studio?

LLOYD: I couldn't really say for sure; they're certainly good enough. I don't know why he doesn't use them all the time. I think that it was probably a producer's decision. But, from what I understand, he pretty much controls what he does. I think what he probably does, is that he probably does it to keep them involved, but it's probably quicker using the studio [session] guys.

BEGO: That is what I assumed, that scheduling-wise, it was probably easier to use musicians who are always in Nashville and do that all of the time for a living.

LLOYD: And those guys, from what I understand, will also play dates on their own when he's not with them, so it's probably a question of scheduling, because they might not want to take that time off themselves, and just not be working. . . . They play a lot of dates on the road [without George], and that's got a lot to do with it.

BEGO: Do you feel that he was really ahead of the pack in stripping away the pop influences that were taking over country music in the late '70s and early '80s?

LLOYD: Well, as I said, he was the first real . . . Well, you know there was a big backlash against the *Urban Cowboy* thing . . .

BEGO: In Nashville?

LLOYD: Yes, very much so.

BEGO: The album went Platinum, and . . .

LLOYD: Again, I was involved with the guy who was really at the forefront of that. Johnny Lee was someone I produced over the years. . . . The difference with that was that it was part of a movement as opposed to the personality. Johnny had all sorts of Number One hits and yet never really attained the status that I think warranted his Number One hits. And, I think it was because people felt—the "old guard," or whatever you wanted to call them—just felt that that wasn't really *country music*. I beg to differ on that, and I think it was. I think that it was just a question of making it a little more "pop." Nashville's really a closed kind of a town, and I think what happened is that when the *Urban Cowboy* thing came about, a lot of outsiders started coming in, and Nashville sort of closed its doors to that. Nashville, particularly at that time, was very provincial. So, when George Strait came along, people greeted him with open arms, because he was really going back to the roots.

BEGO: Well, the *Urban Cowboy* thing, the album's success, was based as much on the country music of Johnny Lee, and Charlie Daniels, as it was The Eagles, Boz Scaggs, Linda Ronstadt and Bonnie Raitt being on the album.

LLOYD: Exactly. What's amazing about that is that the flip side of [the single version of Johnny Lee's] "Looking for Love" was an Eagles' song, not even a Johnny Lee song. I think the *Urban Cowboy* thing really happened by accident. No one really expected it, and "Looking for Love" [by Johnny Lee] was completely by accident. They all thought that Mickey Gilley would be the star coming out of that movie; it was Johnny Lee. Johnny Lee became it, and unfortunately, he couldn't really handle it. . . .

BEGO: You mean the pressure of sudden fame?

LLOYD: Yeah. He got into drugs, and into thinking that he was a real "star." George Strait never did that. He just stayed *straight.* . . . Everybody just liked him, and he's always been real laid back, and just a good guy. There hasn't been a hint of scandal about him. . . . And he isn't a publicity hound at all, he's very humble, and again—every record he has put out is either Number One, or the lowest he had was . . . and I'm looking at the [chart figures] book right now . . . was right after "Unwound," which went to Number Six. And after that, everything is in the Top Five. . . . Right up to this year, "Check Yes or No." Again, George Strait's track record is amazing. Randy Travis, they [his record company] are literally fighting to bring back.

BEGO: Why is it that Randy Travis is so welded into the 1980s, and George Strait is as current as ever?

LLOYD: I don't know for sure. I think there was some adverse publicity about him, relative to who he married, that she has been calling all of the shots. There was always a controversy about whether or not he was really as nice a guy as they made him out to be. With Randy Travis, they didn't believe it, whereas with George Strait they *did* believe it. And that is the big difference. George Strait has never had that kind of a thing. His marriage seems excellent, and he just seems like such a nice, humble kind of guy. There is just a real difference there.

BEGO: It seems like in the early '80s, Nashville was welcoming in a lot of new people. For instance, Alabama really brought the concept of a country/rock band to Nashville, trailblazing the way for Restless Heart, Sawyer Brown, and The Mavericks. Do you think that in this way, George Strait really hit it off in Nashville well? He seemed to hit all of the right keys along these lines: he's a married man, he had kids, no drug problem, no run-ins with the law. Do you think that these factors helped him?

LLOYD: Yeah, I think that that was a really big factor. I think that over the years, it is interesting—and I was thinking about it again just the other day—that to this day they are still cloning George Strait.

BEGO: They really are, because I think, without George Strait, there wouldn't be an Alan Jackson or Clint Black. . . .

LLOYD: Right, because all of these acts—the "hat acts"—wouldn't exist. They are all clones of George Strait. They are still doing it to this day. It's real interesting to me, because I would venture to say that if he came out today, and tried to get a record deal today, and nobody knew him, I think he'd have a hard time getting a deal. Because, there are so many people who sound like him, and they're still cloning him. I wouldn't say he's a "great" singer. He's a "good" singer. But he's pleasant, and he's a good-looking guy. And what they're doing now is coming up with twenty-two-, twenty-three-, twenty-four-year-old kids who are all imitations of him, and most of them don't stick, again, because he's the original. But, as I said, if he would try to come out today, he would have a hard time, which is interesting, because actually he was the first one, but today they would say, "Well, he's just like so and so."

BEGO: How do you think his movie has impacted his career? Do you think it has added a new dimension?

LLOYD: I don't think it was very meaningful one way or another. I really don't. . . . I don't think it had any impact. I don't think it was a great movie. I don't think anyone cared one way or the other.

BEGO: Well, it did give him his biggest selling album ever.

LLOYD: Yeah, it was a big-selling album, but I don't think it had a huge impact one way or another.

BEGO: Do you think that it introduced his music to a movie-going audience who wouldn't have normally been exposed to it, and might not normally buy a country album?

LLOYD: I don't think so.

BEGO: To what do you attribute his long-term success? Because he seems to have the uncanny ability to pick . . .

LLOYD: . . . great songs! I think he knows his audience, and I think he picks them himself, where a lot of guys let other people pick them. And the fact that he has always been the coproducer of his records, and I think he's really concerned with what he sings. He always sings songs that are very clean. They are never controversial.

BEGO: Right, and he never gets into political issues.

LLOYD: And, he's never tried to cross over into pop. A lot of these people do, and then have resistance. He's never done that. He's always remained true to what he does, and what he sells. He knows what he can do, and he never goes away from it. And, I think that's got a lot to do with it.

BEGO: It seems like he only shows up in Nashville to go to the awards shows, or to record his albums, and then goes right straight home to Texas. In this way, is he viewed as an outsider?

LLOYD: No. He's not part of the woodwork, and that adds part of his appeal.

BEGO: He's not at every opening or industry party.

LLOYD: Exactly, he's considered more of a "star," and I think that really helps him, as opposed to being here [in Nashville] all the time.

BEGO: You never see him showing up and doing guest spots on [TV's] *Home Improvement,* or anything like that.

LLOYD: No, and I think that that is very smart. I think his management is very smart in the way they handle him— very, very smart. In fact, in my mind, I thought the movie was kind of a mistake. But, the soundtrack did very well, yet I don't think the movie was very good. Although, I don't think that the movie had a negative effect. I don't think it had an overly positive effect either.

BEGO: One of the things that he hasn't done, that it seems like everyone else has done, is that he stays away from doing videos. He hates doing videos.

LLOYD: Well, he did one for "Check Yes or No". . . .

BEGO: Yes, he must have finally been talked into it, though. He did one maybe ten years ago [*You Look So Good in Love*], and reportedly hated it so much, he had it pulled off the air. However after his movie, I think that he was finally forced into it. Do you think that videos are necessary for breaking hits in Nashville today?

LLOYD: I think now it is. I think for new people it really is. I think in his case, what he does—I think he has the attitude that Conway Twitty had for a long time, that too much exposure is not good, and I think that's what he stays away from. I think that has been a big help to him. . . . A lot of people overexpose themselves; after a while you get sick of seeing them all the time. And, I don't think he's done that. I think he picks really good songs, and again, he tours so much that I think that's what he feels is more important than doing the videos. But I think that in breaking new acts, it very necessary.

BEGO: Well, it seems like ten years after the MTV formula was developed for breaking acts via video, country music is in the throes of this formula: if you don't look good on video, forget about a record deal.

LLOYD: Right, you're not gonna get signed. Today it's totally look oriented. The thing about George Strait is . . . what's really helped him a lot is that he is a good-looking guy, and clean-cut-looking guy. I don't know what he does, but he sure hasn't aged very much.

BEGO: He's forty-four now, and he looks about the same as when he first hit it big in his twenties. Do you think, conversely, that— someone who has been overexposed: Billy Ray Cyrus—that this opposite formula has hurt him? Would you say that the way Billy Ray's career has unfolded is the exact opposite strategy?

LLOYD: I would say that he is a great example of that. I think Tanya Tucker is a good example. I think Reba [McEntire] is a good example. Dolly Parton is another good example. I think having a TV show and all of this sort of stuff has killed these people. Barbara Mandrell is a good example—in fact, Barbara Mandrell is probably the best example of overexposure killing your career.

BEGO: She's never quite recovered from that mega-exposure that her TV series brought her. The TV show was her peak, and after that, she appears to be floundering.

LLOYD: It's hard to get work after that happens. George Strait has never done that, and he is very selective about what shows he appears on. You don't see him that much; yet he's always Number One, and he's always nominated for Entertainer of the Year.

BEGO: If you were given the bridle to steer his career for the next year, what would you do, and what would you suggest he do?

LLOYD: I'd just keep cutting great songs. . . . That's all I would do, and I would be real selective about whatever video he did, and I would just keep touring. That's all I would do, and I wouldn't do anything else. I don't think I'd do any more movies, though. He's not an actor.

BEGO: He was really playing himself. Colonel Tom Parker, Elvis Presley's manager, is one of the people instrumental in talking him into it. It's kind of funny that *Pure Country* is loosely based on Elvis' second film, *Loving You.*

LLOYD: I hadn't really thought about that, but that's actually true. . . . I think again, that if he [George] were to look back on it, he would think that the movie was a mistake. . . . I don't think you'll be seeing him do it again—at least in my own mind. . . . But again, [he's had] an amazing run. I mean, for fifteen years, to be having Number One hits. I don't think anybody realizes that it's that long.

BEGO: What is amazing, too, is that the boxed set has sold three million copies, and is the top-selling boxed set in country music history, and most of the stuff on it has been released before, yet it is still on the charts. It's like people can't get enough of him. Again, because he's not over-exposed, and I think that his old songs still hold up next to his new material.

LLOYD: Yeah, I think he's cutting good songs, always. I think there were a couple of songs that were really kind of crappy, like "Lovebug." I never quite understood why he did that.

BEGO: It's a totally silly song, and it was embarrassingly stupid the first time around when George Jones recorded it.

LLOYD: Yeah, but it still went Number One. You know what I mean? I think that is a great example of a guy who can go to Number One with a shitty song, because that was a shitty song. But I think that that last song that he just did, "Check Yes or No," has gotten tremendous acclaim, and any damage that any songs did before that, I think this one eliminated that problem. It has been such a huge song, and a huge video. What a great song—a great, great song. I think that the other thing that he does, is that he sings what he can sing. You see a lot of guys record a lot of things that they don't sound believable on, and he's never done that. I think that his vocal ability is limited, and that he is good at what he does; but if he tried to do something different, he wouldn't cut it. And, it's knowing what you do well.

BEGO: One of his big passions is the songs of Bob Wills & His Texas Playboys. Do you foresee him doing a tribute album to them? Would that be a good idea in your mind?

LLOYD: No, I don't think so. I think that would be too limited. I think again, that his songs, like "All My Ex's Live in Texas," "Ocean Front Property," and "Does Fort Worth Ever Cross Your Mind," and "Amarillo by Morning," and things like that—and "The Fireman" obviously—I think that he's just always picked great songs. So, personally, I think that would be a mistake.

BEGO: This gives me a great perspective from a Nashville insider, who is involved in the music business, and is familiar with country music totally from the inside.

LLOYD: Well, he is someone who is very respected, in every sense of the word. And, there is no jealousy about him. Whereas, with other guys, who've come along—like when you mentioned Billy Ray Cyrus—there's a guy who fought an uphill battle, and people just wanted to see him fail, and of course he has. I think that there's a lot of people who felt the same way about Travis, because . . .

BEGO: Randy Travis, as opposed to Travis Tritt?

LLOYD: Yes, because his management pissed on a lot of people. . . . And, I think the same thing is true with Cyrus' people, when they started asking for incredible prices [for his appearances], and some of the [TV] specials, some of them were embarrassing. Now, again, he made a fortune. And if he put his money away in the right things, he's . . .

BEGO: . . . set for life . . .

LLOYD: Yeah . . . got the last laugh, and is set for life. But the problem, I think, with a lot of these people is that their ego doesn't allow them to stop. And whereas, as an example, I've told Johnny Lee, "I think you'd be better off just forgetting about it, as opposed to playing gigs for a thousand dollars and two thousand dollars." But he didn't know anything else, and didn't manage his money well, so consequently, that's what he's out doing. I think Strait probably—and I don't know this—but I would imagine he's handled his money quite well.

BEGO: He owns property, and doesn't seem to be doing anything too wild.

LLOYD: When the time comes, I would think—my prognosis for him would be—when he stops having big records, that he would stop. I don't think that he is going to allow himself to go into the mid-chart or low-chart range, and fight it out, like Barbara Mandrell did, and people like that, or Dolly Parton—who tries to desperately hang on, and radio will just not accept them. But again, you would think that by now radio would be resisting him, but in no way is that happening.

BEGO: Have you met him?

LLOYD: I've met him a couple of times, but nothing very significant. But everyone who knows him just speaks incredibly highly of him. And, of course, as you know, his manager was at MCA Records, Erv Woolsey, and left MCA just to manage him. And, obviously, he did a great job.

BEGO: He's doing an excellent job.

LLOYD: Oh, yeah, they are pressing all the right buttons, which is strange, because most people screw up at some point. In his case, I can't really point to anything, and he's never had a scandal. I think that's probably the biggest factor with him. Because, everybody has had something . . .

BEGO: . . . a drinking problem, or wife beating, or . . .

LLOYD: . . . Everybody has got something. He's never had anything. And if he has, they certainly have kept it under wraps.

BEGO: The worst thing that has happened is the death of his daughter . . .

LLOYD: Yeah, but that was a tragedy. If anything, that . . . in a lot of ways, he handled that so well that the public embraced him even more because he didn't do anything real maudlin about it. I think that everything with him is classy, and he handles himself with a lot of class. A lot of acts have it, and a lot of them don't. Nashville is still trying to clone him every day, and without a lot of success. Because these guys have these short little runs, and then they are gone.

BEGO: And there are even more of them as time goes by, making it even more diluted.

LLOYD: Absolutely. I mean, the cowboy hat, with him it's natural. But a lot of these people, honestly, I just want to go over and rip the hat off of their heads, and say, "What are you doing, man?"

BEGO: That's true, George Strait is the real item.

LLOYD: He is the real item—he *is* a cowboy, he really is: came from Texas, the whole routine. Self-taught, and everything. He's just a "straight shooter"; that is just the best way to put it! And, a really interesting guy.

Chapter Twelve

"Cyber Strait"

Another vantage point that is important to explore when painting a portrait of George Strait is the perspective of his fans and his public. These are truly the people who make his career tick. I decided to seek out his ultimate fan and found him on the Internet. His name is Troy Sniff, and he lives in Colorado. Not only is he an admirer of George's and of the Strait sound of his music, but he is also a team roping rodeo cowboy who has attended the "George Strait Team Roping Classic" and all of its related events. Troy created and maintains the "George Strait Home Page" on the Internet. [It can be accessed on the World Wide Web, by running a "George Strait" search in "Web Crawler," or any of several other Internet retrieval programs.]

Like David Daily, Troy Sniff is a businessman by day, and he enjoys surfing cyberspace in his free time. It seemed natural for him to create a Web Page about his favorite country singer. Thousands of people have logged onto Troy's informative "George Strait Home Page" since it

debuted in 1995. The "George Strait Home Page" has
several different side pages that can be accessed from the
main page. Among them is one about the "Jenifer Strait
Memorial Fund," which informs fans about the fund, how
to contribute, and gives information on what charitable
work the money ultimately goes toward. Among the people
whom Troy has personally heard from are George and
Norma Strait themselves. In the summer of 1996 I had a
fascinating conversation with Troy Sniff about George, the
Team Roping Classic, and his Web Page:

BEGO: Tell me about the team roping event. What was it
like? This was something that you'd read about and heard
about for quite some time. . . .

SNIFF: Yes, I've known about it for quite some time, but
I was never actually in the area, or close to where it takes
place, [which is] Kingsville, Texas, in the second weekend
in June.

BEGO: What was it like?

SNIFF: Well, I'm a team roper, so I enjoy team roping,
plus I got to watch some of the best team ropers in the
world rope. All of the top team ropers were out there.
Well, not all of them, but some of the best ones in the
world were out there, so it was nice for me to get to watch
some of them do their thing. . . . Plus I got to take some
real good pictures of George in concert afterwards. I hadn't
taken a vacation in a long time, so I decided to take my
vacation down there, in Kingsville, Texas, at the Team
Roping Classic.

BEGO: What is Kingsville like?

SNIFF: Hot, dusty, dry, with gray dirt. The minute you get out of the shower, you're sweating already. It's not a place that I would like to live. But, you get in some areas and it's really clean, and it was nice where they were holding the Team Roping Classic, and where they hold the barbecue and all, which was at a local club. Tara and all of them, they sat out for the concert. They got there, I believe at 11:00 P.M. the night before. Tara Butkovick ... was the one who helped me get to the Team Roping Classic, and suggested places to stay down there. She's a real nice girl, and right now she's helping me on the Web Page. She's handling the "guest book," and sending out welcome letters and all, because I just couldn't do it anymore.

BEGO: George's role in the event: is he just one of the competitors? Is he the emcee or announcer, or is he just one of the riders?

SNIFF: No, his wife and his brother's wife are actually the ones who go through all of the work of setting it up. Of course he puts on the George Strait Team Roping Classic, but all day he's just one of the crowd. He walks around back there with the team ropers. When it's his turn to rope, he just gets up and ropes, and when he's done, he just goes back to doing the normal thing. The only difference is that he has to put on a concert later that night.

BEGO: So, at the team roping event he's not signing autographs or hanging out with his friends; he's just strictly there as a rodeo rider?

SNIFF: As far as I know, from what I saw.... He was in the booth just walking around, and he'd come down when it was time for him to ride. He was just talking to people, but I'm not sure if he was signing autographs or not.

BEGO: But he wasn't doing a "star trip" at all?

SNIFF: No, he wasn't on a star trip at all. When he goes out there, he's just basically one of the guys. He goes out there and ropes with them, and joins with them.

BEGO: Do things start early in the day, or do things start at noon, or . . .?

SNIFF: I think it was around 9:00 A.M. that the team roping started.

BEGO: And they go on until when?

SNIFF: I think it was about 3:30 P.M. on Friday. And Saturday it was a little earlier, around 1:30, but I couldn't really say. I didn't pay exact attention. . . . It started in the morning, and ended up in the early afternoon.

BEGO: It was held on both Friday and Saturday?

SNIFF: Friday is when everybody ropes, and Saturday is pretty much the finals. . . . Friday night there was a barbecue. It was "Strait, Aces, and a Flush," was the name of the casino night. It was held at a club and basically . . . you paid twenty dollars for [an] all-you-can-eat barbecue. They gave you a bunch of gambling chips, which you could go and gamble with and, if you won more chips, you could gamble them for Team Roping Classic merchandise. So there were a lot of people, and they had different tables all over the place. It was just kind of like for fun gambling—not actually for money, but for prizes. They had different things like a singing competition. Actually, a friend of Tara's won it. Basically, a bunch of people went up there and sang a George Strait song, and the crowd voted to decide who was the winner. . . . It was pretty much a fun thing for everybody. . . . There was no music. They just got up there and sang on their own. I had a great time, because I met a lot of people who were from the Web Pages, and I met people from all over the United States who had nothing to do with the Web Page. On the Thursday night before the Team Roping Classic, they had a George Strait fan meeting at the Country Luau, a little country bar right in Kingsville. There were a bunch of people there, and they talked a little bit about George and what was going on, and what he was doing next, and what the Team Roping Classic was all about. And, they gave out tickets for prizes, and called out different raffle numbers; and prizes were given out, including tickets for the Team Roping Classic, tee shirts, ball caps. They weren't all George Strait items, but also Bud Light items. I have a hat I got, and a George Strait tee shirt.

BEGO: Were those kinds of items also available for purchase?

SNIFF: Right. Everything wasn't all focused around George, but Bud Light rodeo as well . . .

BEGO: Were they a sponsor?

SNIFF: Right. His last year sponsor [1995] was Bud Light, so I believe that they were sponsoring the Team Roping Classic, too.

BEGO: Was there a concert that evening at a club?

SNIFF: No, it was just a fun get-together. The concert was on the Saturday night. It was the get-together on Thursday, the barbecue on Friday, and the concert on Saturday night.

BEGO: Was the Thursday get-together a welcoming party event?

SNIFF: When we got there on Thursday, it was a "Welcome to Kingsville, Texas," and they said something about Kleberg County Parks and Recreation, because they were the ones who held the George Strait Team Roping Classic, along with George and his brother, and his family and all.

BEGO: Was George there?

SNIFF: No, he wasn't.

BEGO: Was Saturday's concert basically for people who had tickets to the Team Roping Classic, or was it open to the public apart from the rodeo events?

SNIFF: Not necessarily.

BEGO: You could buy tickets just for the concert?

SNIFF: Yes, you could just go to the concert if you wanted to. The rodeo tickets from Friday were different from the rodeo tickets for Saturday. The Classic tickets and the concert tickets were completely separate.

BEGO: How much were the tickets to the Classic?

SNIFF: The team roping tickets I believe were seven dollars apiece. . . . I ended up paying thirty-five dollars for the concert and both days of the team roping. I believe it was thirty-five dollars, but it may have been less than that. Let me find the ticket stubs; I think they are right here. [pause] I have a whole box full of memorabilia here . . . okay, here they are: it was six dollars for the team roping events each day. It was thirty-two dollars total, so it was twenty dollars for the concert on Saturday.

BEGO: Well, that's quite the bargain. Let's talk about your George Strait Web Page. What inspired it? Was it something that you came up with after that? What made you want to do this?

SNIFF: No, I started the Web Page a long time before this. . . . I started the Web Page originally around November 21, 1995. [It's called] "The George Strait Home Page."

BEGO: How can people contact it?

SNIFF: They can just do a "George Strait" search, and it will show up on "Web Crawler," or one of the other search programs, and they will find the "George Strait Home Page." It is the largest one. There are only two George Strait pages involving George Strait. There are other pages where he is just mentioned.

BEGO: There are also the official record company bios you can pull up . . .

SNIFF: Yes, MCA Records has their own little site on George Strait, and then there is another guy, by the name of Joe Combes, with a "George Strait Fan Page," and then I have the only actual "George Strait Home Page" on the Internet.

BEGO: Have you talked to a lot of people since setting this up?

SNIFF: The numbers right now are around 66,000 people who have pulled it up so far. I can't tell you exactly how many of them have signed the "guest book," but quite a few. I'm on the twentieth page right now, and there are over a hundred per page. I've never really gone in and tried to count them all.

BEGO: That's quite impressive!

SNIFF: I started it basically because I was playing on the Internet and I wanted to see what it would be like to build a home page on the Internet. I did a search on my favorite country artist—George Strait—and Joe Combes had his. . . . It listed his albums and some other information, but it didn't have any background information. So, I had wanted to build a Web Page, so I figured, "Why not build a Web Page on my favorite artist?" So, that's how that got started. . . . I started it up small, and then I began to build it up. A bunch of my friends on the Internet took a look at it, and said to me, "You really ought to carry it on." And they said, "Put it in the Search, and register it in the Search." So I did, and I started getting quite a few people coming in. And this was before I really started logging in or counting the number of people coming in. People kept leaving me messages: "Are you going to continue it, and add more information to it, and make it larger?" So, I did it. . . . At one point I was adding a little bit more to it by the day. It became hard for me to continue to keep track of the names on the "guest book." I had to make sure that there weren't any improper entries, or foul language— because I know that there are lots of children who log onto the Internet. I don't put any information on the Home Page that is too personal, because I know what George does and does not want people to know publicly— and that's his family life. Almost all of my information ends up being public information that has been published somewhere else, so that it only contains information he wouldn't mind the public knowing. I think the biggest thing that I like about the page is that I created the Memorial Page for the Jenifer Strait Memorial Fund. Because, a lot of people didn't know what it was, so it gave it a little bit more exposure. I couldn't tell you right off the bat how many people have donated money because of that Web Page, but I can tell you that I did get a letter from George Strait and his wife, thanking me for creating that Web Page.

BEGO: It's nice to know that they are impressed with what you have done.

SNIFF: Would you like me to read it to you?

BEGO: Positively, I'm curious to find out what they wrote.

SNIFF: It has the "George Strait" logo on the top, and it is dated April 25, 1996. It says:

Dear Mr. Sniff:

Thank you for your donation to the Jenifer Strait Memorial Foundation, and for creating a George Strait Home Page on the Internet to help others to have the opportunity to contribute. The earnings of the foundation are used to support children's charities. Some of the organizations that have benefited have been the San Antonio Baptist Children's Home, the San Antonio Police Department's Drug and Alcohol Abuse Program, and Youth Alternatives, Incorporated—an organization that supports abused and neglected children and youth. Because of your thoughtfulness on behalf of Jenifer's memory, and the charities that will benefit, is greatly appreciated.

Sincerely,

Norma & George Strait

BEGO: And they both signed it?

SNIFF: Yes, the letter's typed and signed. I couldn't tell you if it was Norma's handwriting, or George's, but it is personally signed.

BEGO: That is so consistent with everything that I've learned about George. Between the team roping, the Web Page, and your dedication to George Strait, you are a wealth of information. Is there anything else you'd like to add?

SNIFF: Well, I have to say, the best thing about seeing George in concert down at the Team Roping Classic is that that was probably the best time I had ever seen him in concert. And everybody told me that it probably would be, because, obviously he was enjoying himself. He was doing something he loved, and he seemed a lot more relaxed onstage up there. He looked like he had a lot more fun than most of his other concerts that I've been to. I've loved all of his concerts, but this particular night was probably the best concert of George's. His show seemed to be a little bit longer, and he put a little more into it. It seemed like he just had more fun with it, because he was relaxed, and he'd had a great day—I'm sure—doing what he loves, and that's team roping. He probably doesn't get to do that much, because he's always on the road. Everybody told me, "You're gonna see the best concert if you go to see him at the Team Roping Classic." He's a lot more relaxed, he's a lot more laid back, and he seemed a lot happier. He doesn't get to spend a lot of time with his family, and I'm sure that has a lot to do with it. While they were taking pictures after the Classic, and before the concert that night, he was out there joking with everybody, and joking with his family, joking with his son. His son was walking around, and the girls were screaming his son's name, and things like that. And they just looked like they were having a good time. They weren't exactly playing the celebrity act, I guess you could say. They were just trying to enjoy themselves. At least that's the way it came off to me. Nowhere, anytime, did he look like he was trying to be "George Strait"; he was just trying to be somebody enjoying himself, doing what he likes to do. That's the way it came across to me.

BEGO: That's pretty consistent with what I know about him.

SNIFF: Every concert I've been to, I've never seen him in a concert where it looks like he doesn't want to be up there. I've enjoyed every show. A lot of people say that he doesn't put on as good a show as others, because he's not real active onstage. But that's what George Strait is all about, but that's just my personal opinion. I like him for his music. I don't like an artist for his getting up and running around onstage and swinging on ropes and things like that. I listen to the music. I don't go there to worship a person. I go there to listen to the music. And, if he's just up there right in front of the microphone and just sings all night, as long as he sings the songs the way that I like them, that's fine with me. He doesn't try to put on anything he's not just to impress his fans or make his fame.

BEGO: That's great!

SNIFF: That's George Strait.

Chapter Thirteen

"Strait Talk: A Critical View"

Having spoken to someone from George's past (David Daily), a Nashville insider (Mick Lloyd), and one of his biggest admirers (Troy Sniff), the time had come to take a critical look at his music and his career. I turned to two New York City music critics, Marcy MacDonald, and Gino Falzarano; a Tucson rodeo promoter and Strait fan, George Plentzas; and a Los Angeles music and social critic, Angela Bowie. This would successfully enable us to take a look at and examine George Strait's career from both coasts, and from the genuine Wild West cowboy country as well.

TOO STRAIT?
An Interview with Marcy MacDonald,
New York City, August 10, 1996

"Is George Strait too straight for his own good?" asks noted New York arts critic Marcy MacDonald. She has been touched by Strait's music in a way that has caused her to exclaim, "Even hard-bitten New Yorkers know and love George Strait's music. Even the snobbiest Manhattanites realize that Nashville isn't just a town in Tennessee, just like we all know that 'denial' isn't a river in Egypt. George Strait continues to make his mark in the Big Apple in a way that most other country singers only dream of doing.

"Given George Strait's background, and his roots in the heart of Texas, it isn't all that amazing to find that he has become the main man and the mainstay of traditionalist country music as we know it today. The fact that he eloped with his high school sweetheart and first became interested in country music while on an army base in Hawaii all added new dimensions to his personality, and made him appreciate his Texas roots even more. He took his amateur home-base-grown experiences in Hawaii and perfectly applied his band-leading expertise into the band we now know as Ace in the Hole. His interest in Bob Wills & His Texas Playboys, alone, brought their incredible swing sound into the '80s and '90s. We might never have fully appreciated country swing in this decade if it wasn't for George Strait. He did the same thing for Bob Wills and Texas swing that Bonnie Raitt has done for her idol Sippie Wallace ['You Got to Know How'] and the blues. He made it current, and kept it alive.

"His consistent trail of having recorded twenty-one Gold or Platinum albums is legendary in the record business, especially in the country field where careers seem to peak and burn out so quickly. Look at Billy Ray Cyrus. By contrast, George has all of the consistency and the staying power without ever having done the 'Achy Breaky' dance!

"As an interviewer, I know how private he is. Most country singers will show up at a public event for the opening of an envelope. The annual country music awards shows are just about the only times he surfaces—aside from his concerts. I remember when all of us celebrity reporters wanted to be the first one to get him to open up about the death of his daughter, Jenifer. Here it is, ten years later, and he is still protecting his privacy steadfastly. It is really out of respect for him that the press has completely laid off of using that angle whenever they write about him.

"I was personally curious as to whether or not he was going to address the car accident that took her away, in his music. He has never acknowledged that tragic event in his music. Eric Clapton, of course, took the exact opposite tack when he wrote the song 'Tears in Heaven' about the death of his young son. George just shut down all systems for a year. He just turned down all opportunities to discuss it in any way. Because of his silence, everyone wanted to know who was driving the car and what the exact circumstances surrounding the accident were. Instead of bugging him, the press simply allowed him to grieve by himself, in the way that he preferred—alone and unbothered by the press. None of us know whether or not he has fully expressed his pain and sense of loss to any—except maybe his wife, Norma. And, as private as he is, we will probably never know exactly how he has expressed his feelings even to her. His innermost feelings are things that he doesn't share with his fans, and he may not even share them with his family. We may never quite know, unless he one day writes his own book—which he keeps refusing to do.

"He is such a natural leader that he is literally directing the direction of country music. The music that he was listening to when he was in high school and college was out of the Johnny Cash, Highwayman, Crystal Gayle, Eddie Rabbitt mode. He completely cut through the pop/rock leanings that country was having at the time and put it on course in the 1980s with his first recordings like 'Unwound,' and 'All My Ex's Live in Texas.' He brought country music right back to his Texas roots. Every album contains one homage to Texas or another, whether it's 'Amarillo by Morning,' 'All My Ex's Live in Texas,' or 'Does

Fort Worth Ever Cross Your Mind,' or his many rodeo songs.

"Although he is a very private guy, he is into sharing his musical talent, and he seems to genuinely enjoy getting a crowd going in concert. There is also the great probability that if he hadn't become a musician, he may have just become a singing rodeo rider. It wasn't the lure of fame that originally drew him to show business; it was his love of the music, and this shines through his entire career and his impressive body of work. From what I know about him, he is completely passionate about his annual team roping competition every June, to the point where he doesn't care if he makes a dime on it. In fact it is his own personal money that keeps it going. That is his passion project.

"George Strait's refusal to give but a few interviews a year has given way to the theory among some that he is hiding some aspect of his personal life. I am completely convinced that George Strait is such a clean-living guy that he makes Debbie Gibson look like a trollop!

"In the 1980s, when Manhattan clubs like Denim & Diamonds became hot, it was songs like George Strait's 'The Fireman' that always got the crowds up out of their seats to dance. I was personally amazed to see how many Texans come to New York, and really get into places like The Lone Star Cafe, and Denim & Diamonds. The recent Central Park concert by Pam Tillis, Carlene Carter, and Lorrie Morgan [summer 1996] was a total smash. New York City is quite aware of country music, and has been ever since George Strait arrived on the scene. Before that, we all turned our noses up at '70s acts like Johnny Paycheck. Between *Urban Cowboy* and George Strait, ever since the 1980s, cowboy hats and cowboy boots have been hot in New York City. They aren't just for life on the ranch now. I think that George Strait is really responsible for pulling country music back to the real Texas values, and for making it one of the hottest segments of the 1990s music scene.

"While, from a celebrity interviewer's aspect, I wish that he would grant more interviews each year, I think that one of the keys to his stronghold at the top of the country music world is the fact that he has never overexposed himself media-wise. He has never had to bare his chest in a country beefcake competition, nor has he made his life an open book just to sell records. And yet, he sells them just the same. Through his music, he shares his sensitivity and his vulnerability with people, and it works. Why tamper with a perfect formula?"

REDEFINING THE COWBOY IMAGE
An Interview with Gino Falzarano, New York City, August 14, 1996

Gino Falzarano is a music archivist and New York based critic, whose writing has appeared in several publications including the record collector's bible, *Discoveries*. According to Gino, "As a New York music critic, I am not necessarily into country music per se, yet the wide musical appeal of George Strait has made me a country fan. It's not so much the sound. The sound in itself is not unique; what he brings to country—or to music in general—is the imagery. My favorite song of his, 'Amarillo by Morning,' presents the musical scenario of the cowboy as loner. The cowboy who maybe doesn't see the writing on the wall, who is breaking bones, losing wives, girlfriends, whatever, because of the lifestyle he has chosen. The rodeo is the only thing that he knows, the only thing that he enjoys. What shines through all of George Strait's music is the imagery, and the mystique of the American cowboy.

"In real life, we all know that George really loves the rodeo, and his life on horseback, as a rodeo rider. It's basically the cowboy as loner that seems to shine through all of his songs. Right up to 1996, the song 'I Can Still Make Cheyenne' from his *Blue Clear Sky* album, George constantly reinforces this lonesome rodeo cowboy persona in his music. He perpetuates the image of the West, and the roadside saloon. There is almost an innocence to the whole lifestyle of the cowboy. And, as opposed to so many of the singers in Nashville today, George Strait is a real cowboy, not just someone who has put on a cowboy hat and is pretending to be a cowboy.

"You can't compare him to a singer like Alan Jackson, because there are two opposite things happening there. I feel that Alan Jackson is almost the *Urban Cowboy* type of performer, especially on his songs 'Don't Rock the Jukebox' and 'Midnight in Memphis.' He just hits all of the right buttons to create the mood by mentioning Hank Williams, and George Jones, but they still come across as connect-the-dots kind of songs. But with George Strait, there is no question that he is the real item.

"For Alan Jackson, it was almost impossible for those songs to go wrong, because they went so far to suggest the country/cowboy lifestyle by mentioning the Opry, the South, and so many country music references. In my mind, those songs don't have the same heart and soul that 'Amarillo by Morning' or even 'All My Ex's Live in Texas' possess. So many country hits like Jackson's 'Chattahoochie' and Billy Ray Cyrus' 'Achy Breaky Heart' try so hard to be cute and clever. While all of this is going on, George just slips in with 'Blue Clear Sky' or 'Heartland,' and the idea of a cowboy on horseback immediately pops into your mind.

"George Strait's songs really have legs. They work. They worked ten years ago; they will work twenty years from now. There is a timeless quality to them. Listen to 'Amarillo by Morning,' and you'll hear a great song—not just a great country song, but a great song *period*. As with so many of his songs, he creates music that you can go back to, and really get lost in.

"There are a lot of fun, country, party songs like Alan's 'Chattahoochie' or Tim McGraw's 'Indian Outlaw,' which are perfect for the dance floor, where you just need a good melody to two-step or line dance to, but George Strait's songs are the kind of music you can really sit and listen to time and time again. The imagery is all there, and his music evokes a mood, and an era, and a lifestyle that is completely unique. There are a lot of totally disposable country songs out there, but George Strait's music is truly here to stay!

"George's songs are really solid songs. The musicianship is very strong, and the Ace in the Hole band is great on-stage. George's whole image and the way he is packaged is, in my mind, the way that country is supposed to be, without all of the frills that so many '90s country stars surround themselves with. To me, country is about a man and his guitar, singing about his life and his often-lonely lifestyle, with his horse, under the stars. That simplicity is very appealing, especially in the complicated 1990s. For me, George Strait is the ultimate country star, and everything he does reinforces his likable cowboy image and represents the key and the foundation to his enduring widespread appeal."

NO FRILLS STRAIT
An Interview with George Plentzas,
Tucson, August 11, 1996

George Strait expert and local Tucson, Arizona, rodeo promoter George Plentzas has been avidly following Strait's career throughout the 1990s. According to him, it was mainly Strait's music that catapulted him into the country music scene in general. "Unlike Brooks & Dunn, or

Garth Brooks—who have a stage full of props and lights whenever they perform in concert—the key to George Strait's music is just standing there and just playing great music. I was startled the first time that I saw George perform here in Tucson. I had no expectations as to the visual appearance of the show, but I was surprised that for his stage set— there was no set! There was a flat stage with the guitars, the amps and all of the mikes, and that was it. There was nothing to give it the ambiance of a country show: no split rail fences, no pickup trucks, no risers, nothing. There were, of course, a few lights and pieces of technical equipment, but nothing like you would imagine that some of the major country stars use these days.

"On the other side of the fence, there is Garth Brooks, who has absolutely everything imaginable—from smoke and mirrors to a spaceship. Then there is Brooks & Dunn, who have a gigantic cattle skull. One of Vince Gill's recent stage sets had a complete library of books and a car, like he was performing with a garage band in an actual garage— complete with attic. Then there is Reba, who has a two-tiered stage, with different levels which rotate and change while she is standing on it, with elevators and well over a dozen members of her back-up band, and everything. In contrast, George Strait was just about the music, pure and simple.

"You would think that—after seeing some of these other performers in the same arena, Tucson Convention Center—that the audience would be disappointed that the stage was so stark and simple. However, the second that he hit the stage, the roar of the audience was overwhelming. From the moment the Ace in the Hole band took the stage before George, there was an excitement that ran through the crowd that was incomparable. I've seen Garth Brooks, and he certainly knows how to get a crowd going, and all of these other performers—just by the sheer power of all of the sights and sounds and staging effects—certainly leave an incredible impression. But, George Strait just gets up there and you get the same ultimate effect—without all of the lights and other distractions. It is all about the music. And, his band is just phenomenal. They came out before him and did a few numbers, and they are great. They are just such talented musicians that the show is flawless from beginning to end. The closest country star has been Alan Jackson, who has had some pretty flashy shows in the past; but on his 1995 tour, he began stripping the stage set down to basics as well, and he did away with all of the cars and trucks that he once had onstage. Alan's sets have been pretty bare lately, but George took it a step even further—and the effect is just as good as if he had a million lights. George Strait is still in a league of his own!

"The music alone is all he needs. The music is good, his band is excellent. He doesn't do a whole lot of talking to the audience; he doesn't do any theatrics at all. And he just gives one hell of a concert! He just gets up there and plays—plays and sings. He and his band just play their hearts out. They want to make sure that you—in the audience—have a good time, and you do!"

THE MARKETING OF GEORGE STRAIT
An Essay by Angela Bowie, Los Angeles, August 24, 1996

Angela Bowie is used to expounding on the wilder side of the music scene. A recording artist, frequent TV talkshow guest, and a social critic, she is also the author of *Backstage Passes*. Her insights never cease to amaze, as she is an expert when it comes to knowledge in the ins and outs of the music industry. She knows firsthand about the marketing machinery that can create a musical media phenomenon. Instead of chatting extemporaneously about George Strait, she composed the following essay:

"There is a fascinating twist to the career and to the legend of George Strait. His enormous popularity and his ability to generate income from album sales and concert tickets is particularly impressive to number counters, and to the tired aficionadoes in this business of music. In the same way that capitalism rewards profit, a financial success, a tried and tested money generator cannot be dismissed. But if one overviews George Strait's career, attempting to find a central key to his charisma—there is none.

"He writes. Though, to hear him tell it, or to listen to his few recorded compositions—not that well. He is gracious and modest enough to acknowledge his good looks and hunk appeal are due to genetics. As he is monogomous and an intensely personal family man, there is little to suggest lust or lasciviousness which— in the rock world—are both prerequisites to fan worship.

"There are many virtuosos, and musical and vocal technocrafters, whose names will be remembered for a while. But, as the legends of Maria Callas and Mario Lanza will attest, many of the music world's biggest stars did not write their own tunes. However, they are both fondly remembered. Callas for her vocal prowess, passion and style, and because she brought Aristotle Onassis to his knees. In an era where industry reveres art, Mario Lanza's claim to fame was for using his operatic voice for contemporary song. But their achievements are appreciated by the few people who got to see them perform and their music publishers. Catalogue is what music is all about. Immortality is about memory. Thus, the interest in George Strait, generated by his film *Pure Country*, is an arena where visuals and music are captured. George Strait and his music are things that will be around for a long time.

"G. K. Chesterton is not remembered as a poet so much as a hymn writer. Memory is money. Capturing memory and turning it into money is the measurement by which capitalists place value on art. Enjoying the music of George

Strait is much like eating an especially good bowl of oat-
meal. It is cuddly to your mind, and it does not challenge
the dark recesses of your psyche. It is clean, wholesome,
uncontroversial, and it is very all-American.

"His music does not give you a stomachache. Rock &
roll: that can give you a stomachache, and getting it played
on American radio was a challenge. Listening to David
Bowie would get you beaten up and get you called a subver-
sive misfit. Listening to The Fugs, Frank Zappa & the Moth-
ers of Invention, and Bob Dylan made you some sort of
anti-American leftist. Disco music labeled you as frivolous,
and punk was equated with drug degeneration. However,
listening to and appreciating George Strait's music: hey—
that's American! It's family, it's roots, it's as acceptable
and as assured as the legends of cowboys and loners. Unlike
the drunken revelries of Willie Nelson and Waylon Jennings in the country realm, George Strait is apple pie at
its finest. He is never out-of-control or scandalous.

"The term 'new traditionalist' is another marketing ploy.
Finding a new way of labeling and marketing a tried and
true product is a challenge. George Strait is not overly
unique, but he is consistently good and, within a certain
realm, predictable. The fact that he is able to enter the
recording studio and churn out million-selling albums
time and time again is admirable and remarkable in today's
totally disposable society. Just like Tide laundry detergent
is perpetually 'new and improved,' year after year, George
Strait rises phoenix-like. He doesn't attempt death-defying
immortality. With Mr. Strait, you know what you are getting
album after album after album, and he never disappoints
his fans. His consistency is remarkable, and his performances are perpetually strong. With George and his music,
what you see and what you hear is what you get: pure
country at its finest. Anyone who can stay at the top of the
stack year after year, like George Strait has, obviously knows
exactly what he is doing, and is doing it well!"

Chapter Fourteen

"Blue Clear Sky"

If you look back at George Strait's career, you can really appreciate how hard he worked to develop a following in his native Texas, to be signed to a record label, to make the jump to a major label, to become a Number One hit maker, and finally to become a bona fide movie star. As difficult as it has been, becoming a singing star is a piece of cake when compared to the task of staying on top for over fifteen years. And that is exactly what George has done.

The times have changed, the hierarchy of Nashville stars has changed, the appeal of country music in the 1990s has changed, and the diverse personalities at the top of the charts have stretched the country music genre to new heights and into new directions. When George was releasing his first singles, there were no beefcake country hunks like Billy Ray Cyrus, there weren't any country/folk singers like Mary-Chapin Carpenter, and there was no such thing as a compact disc. The look, the sound, and the technology of country music have drastically changed since 1981 when

George's _Strait Country_ was originally released as a twelve-inch vinyl album. There was also a completely antiquated system for tallying the sales of records and tapes. Now, in the 1990s thanks to bar coding and computers, _Billboard_ magazine's SoundScan system can tally figures down to how many copies of _Strait Out of the Box_ have sold on a day-to-day basis. But, through it all, one thing hasn't changed one iota: George Strait.

Over fifteen years since the country-listening public first heard the sound of "Unwound" pouring out of their radios, George still wears his cowboy hats and jeans wherever he goes, still refuses to talk about his personal life, and still pumps out one chart-topping hit recording after another. This was witnessed in 1996 when his "Blue Clear Sky" single hit Number One, and the album it came from was certified Platinum. Some things never change.

Hotter than ever, 1995 and 1996 have been two of George's best years yet. In the fall of 1995, George was the third recipient of music publisher ASCAP's Voice of Music Award. He took the prize for his "interpretations of great songs, which have touched the hearts and minds of music lovers throughout the world."

In the fall of 1995, George was at the Hard Rock Cafe in Austin, Texas, for the unveiling of the display of his autographed Gibson Dove guitar. The restaurant paid five thousand dollars to the San Antonio Children's Museum and Children's Shelter for the guitar that Strait donated. It is on permanent display at the restaurant, alongside all of the other rock & roll memorabilia.

In January 1996 music fans were rolling over a story about George lassoing a turkey—a real-live turkey of the Thanksgiving variety. George doesn't know how the story first got around Nashville, but agrees it is true. Apparently he was riding his horse on his ranch in Texas when he spotted something out of the ordinary. Next to a 700-acre field planted with oats was a big tom turkey all by himself.

George wasn't going to bother him, but the turkey flew across the fence. He tried roping the bird a couple of times, and finally had to get off his horse to rope him while running down the fence line. Then George didn't know what to do with him. Since it wasn't November, he just let the turkey go.

Later that month, George and his animals were back in the spotlight. This time it was his dog Buster who was in the news. Buster, George's Australian cattle dog, was missing. The pet was known by Strait's millions of fans. Since his photo appeared on the front cover of the Platinum *Easy Come, Easy Go* album in 1993. To find him, George placed an ad in the *San Antonio Express-News* offering a cash reward for any information leading up to Buster's return.

Although the hurt from the loss of his daughter was never to go away, George had pretty much kept his pain to himself. In 1996, the ten-year anniversary of the establishment of "The Jenifer Strait Memorial Foundation" was nationally announced. Without celebrity events or publicity, George had established the foundation due to the overwhelming outreachings of his fans, after they had heard the tragic news of Jenifer's death. The foundation accepts unsolicited charitable donations and each year channels the funds into several organizations in George's area which help out children in need, including: the San Antonio Baptist Children's Home, the San Antonio Police Department Drug and Alcohol Abuse Program, and Youth Alternative Inc., which aids abused or abandoned kids. [For information contact "The Jenifer Strait Memorial Foundation" c/o Jeff W. Avant, President, P.O. Box 9, Dilley, Texas 78017.] According to the foundation's director, Frank Bohman, "Because of the courage and inspiration of George and Norma Strait, this trust has benefited countless young people in need, while keeping Jenifer's memory alive."

In the spring of 1996, the RIAA (Record Industry Association of America) tallied the sales figures of all of the country stars to appear on the charts. George ranked Number Five on the list, with 22.8 million albums sold as of February 1996. The Number One artist was Garth Brooks at 59 million, trailed by Alabama at 31.5 million, Willie Nelson at 31 million, and Reba McEntire at 25.5 million. True to Strait form, George may not be the flashiest, or the top seller, but like Willie Nelson, he is right in there on the list of the most consistent.

In early 1996, it was business as usual for George. Commencing his 1996 concert tour, he held a brief press conference, stating, "I just want to say it's great to be here in Lexington, Kentucky, to kick off this 1996 tour. It's a new sponsor for me, Chevy Trucks, who I'm very happy to be associated with this year, and hopefully for many years to come. I've been off for about two and a half months, but during that time we've been kinda putting this thing together with a few key Chevy people. It's been a real pleasure to work with 'em, as you can see from the video we've done. We've come up with some other ideas for the year, and I'm looking forward to it."[156]

In April 1996, George's devoted legion of fans were treated to the release of his twenty-first album, *Blue Clear Sky*. Adhering to his recipe for ten-song albums, this latest Platinum seller consists of something old, something new, something borrowed, and something blue.

In the "old" category came Wayne Kemp and Mack Vickery's 1973 composition, "She Knows When You're on My Mind," a bit of classic Nashville, with steel pedal guitars wailing on this sentimental song about a memory that won't go away. In the "something borrowed" column comes the Mark Chesnutt, Roger Springer, Bruce Bouton bouncy and swinging "I Ain't Never Seen No One Like You." And what could better fill out the "blue" category than the title cut itself: "Blue Clear Sky" written by Mark D. Sanders, John Jarrard, and Bob DiPiero [Pam Tillis' husband].

"New" songs—George has plenty on this album, from some of his favorite writers. Dean Dillon and Norro Wilson provided him with the slow and sensitive "Rockin' in the Arms of Your Memory." Aaron Barker and manager Erv Woolsey penned "I Can Still Make Cheyenne," all about a cowboy's passion for the rodeo. Jim Lauderdale and Gary Nicholson gave him the up-tempo "Do the Right Thing." The album ends with the slow and beautiful "Need I Say More," a song of love and devotion.

George's army of fans and devotees not only ran to their local record shops to snap up a million copies of this new album, but it bounced up to the Number One slot in *Billboard* magazine in June. The title song, "Blue Clear Sky," simultaneously sat at the top of the singles charts. George Strait proved once again that he was as hot as ever.

Critic Robert Baird reviewed the album in *New Country* magazine and gave it four stars, glowing, "On *Blue Clear Sky*, Strait continues to deepen and enrich the formula he began back in 1981 on *Strait Country*—mix pop/country tunes with Western swing and traditional country numbers ... If steadiness is a virtue, then George Strait is truly divine. *Blue Clear Sky* is simply Strait doing Strait, which is another way of saying that hat acts have come and gone, but George Strait has outlasted and outclassed them all."[157]

The funny thing was that when the *Blue Clear Sky* album hit Top Country Albums chart in *Billboard*, two of the other seventy-five hot-selling albums on the same chart included his own *Pure Country* (five million copies sold) and his *Strait Out of the Box* (three million copies sold).

On October 2, 1996, George Strait was again in the winner's circle as he won three of the top trophies at the 30th Annual Country Music Association Awards. "Check Yes or No" was named the Single of the Year, "Blue Clear Sky" the Album of the Year, AND George was honored as the Male Vocalist of the Year. For Strait the awards and the accolades never stop!

When he does take a breather and relaxes, whose music does he listen to? "I actually listen to a lot of people," he reveals. "I've always been a big Bob Wills fan. I still love his music, and I still listen to that. I still listen to a lot of Merle Haggard. I listen to Frank Sinatra. I like good singers. I don't care what kind of music they sing. I just like to listen to a real good singer, and I think Sinatra was probably one of the best there ever was."[158]

What about female singers? George grins and says, "We have Terri Clark on our tour this year [1996]. She's up-and-coming, and I think she's really going to be big. I think she's a great singer. I like to listen to Patty Loveless songs a lot. I think she's a great singer, too. I also think Faith Hill is a great singer. There's a lot of them."[159]

With regard to his favorite contemporary male performers George claims, "I listen to Mark Chesnutt and think he's a great singer—and he really does good material. And Alan Jackson: 'Gone Country' was such a great song, great song. My son listens to just about everybody, so I get exposed to all of it."[160]

After all of these years, music is still George's passion. "Music is something that even if I had given it up [professionally] years ago, I probably would still be doing it today. I don't think I could have ever gotten away from it," he says.[161]

When you look at all of the changes in the careers of Reba McEntire and Garth Brooks throughout the years, George remains unwaveringly the same as he ever was. "At times, I get flak for it," he says about his unvarying style. "I read these things and I say, 'What am I supposed to do?' This is what I do. This is the type of music I want to do. What do they want from me, to go out and cut a pop album just to do something different I do country music. I'm a country singer. Good Lord! I just don't understand it when somebody says that."[162]

George's albums pretty much adhere to his same winning formula. Maybe one will have more swing to it, or another one may be ballad heavy, but they are cut from the same cloth. George is the first to argue that there are distinctive differences in each of them. He doesn't think any of his albums are the same. The music is different and each song is different in its own right to him. Some are more traditional than others. If it's a good song and it fits him, he'll sing it.

When a fan of his adds a new George Strait album to his or her collection—whether it is a new release or a catalogue album from the past—they know exactly what they are going to get. In a musical time of uncertainty and experimentation, that is assuring. As long as his albums keep hitting Number One, and his concerts continue to sell out, why knock the formula? Is he in this game for the long haul? "I hope so," he says. "I know I'm going to keep doing it as long as I can, as long as people like it and keep coming out to the shows. I just re-signed with MCA this past year. I've got no intentions of slowing down."[163]

There are several places in America that are strongholds for devotion to George Strait. Tucson, Arizona—the real-life Wild, Wild West—is one such place. Annually, almost without fail, George comes to Tucson and sells out his concert. His shows thrill the audience year after year, keeping them coming back again and again for the great show he delivers. In this one major city (population 750,000 in greater Tucson), here is the overwhelming evidence of consistent demand, and consistent fulfillment. The headlines of Tucson's *Arizona Daily Star* have read: "Crowd Liked Its Country Strait Up" (March 6, 1989), "Strait Gives a Straightforward, Crowd-Pleasing Show" June 10, 1990), "Sold-Out TCC Audience Swings to No-Frills Strait" (June 8, 1992), "It's Strait to the Audience's Heart" (October 10, 1992). The list goes on and on. For George Strait, consistency pays off again and again.

While the satisfying albums and the exciting hit singles

p coming, what more could his fans want? How abo᠁ ᠁ore movies? "Yes, I really enjoyed doing that movie *[Pure Country],*" he says. "It was a lot of fun. I don't have anything planned right now in Hollywood, but it is certainly in the back of my mind! I'm not going to rule anything out right now. Y'see, about the time I did that movie, I started to cut back on some of my concert dates, reason being to have a little more time to spend at home to be with my family. The movie project came up so quickly! It was something we wanted to do, so we did it. But that's one of the reasons why I didn't jump right back into it, because if I do that, it defeats the purpose of cutting down on the concerts. I'd be working more than ever. But then again, I'd have to say, truthfully, if something good comes along, and we have the time to do it after this tour, then we'll jump right in there and do it."[164]

He claims to be pretty happy with the way things are right now. He has the year planned out and to take on a project such as another movie, he'd be back to working the entire year. He's not ready to do that just yet and believes that when he's ready to do another movie, the opportunity will still be available.

It certainly hasn't been a lack of offers that has kept him absent from the silver screen since 1992. He just hasn't been ready to commit to one. This lack of new film productions does not signify retirement for Strait. Quite the opposite in fact. "I don't know where a lot of my fans got the idea that I was on the verge of retiring, but that couldn't be further from the truth," he swears. "I just want them to know that as long as they're going to keep coming to the shows, I'm going to keep coming out there and doing them. So don't think I'm quitting. It's great to have these fans. They're very important, and it's just unbelievable to me that they're still coming out. I just want to say 'thank you' to them."[165]

When it comes to marketing himself, no one does a

finer job than Strait. He has his own line of "C
cowboy hats made by Resistol. George now ex~~~
wears Resistol cowboy hats. He has his own line of p
products available at Kmart stores, too. As far as endorse-
ments go, he has been seen in advertisements for Wrangler
Jeans and Chevy Trucks.

George has a way of keeping himself grounded by
recording his albums, performing in his concerts, and then
returning to the real world back on his ranch in Texas.
According to his longtime manager Erv Woolsey, "George
has a lot of friends where he lives. They're not in the music
business. I think if he made a record that they didn't like,
they'd let him know."[166]

George is still blown away when people single-handedly
credit him with bringing on the reign of traditional country
music into the forefront. He feels complimented when
people say he's been an influence in their career, but
he insists he never set out thinking he'd influence other
people.

It doesn't look like he stands to lose any ground in
that area either. According to his producer, Tony Brown,
"George looks as cool and hip as any of these young twenty-
year-old cats. He just takes care of himself. He's a very
aware individual."[167]

To give an example of just how private he remains, try
asking him how much land he has on his ranch. "In Texas,
that's sort of like bragging about how much money you
have in the bank," he claims. "My daddy brought me up
better than that. But it's a working cattle ranch. I don't
have to think about anything except my cows, my horses,
roping or whatever I want to do. It's a place to relax
and take my mind off the road. The road can get *real*
rough."[168]

In the past fifteen years, George has been pumping out
hits and witnessing all sorts of changes in country music.
"I think country music is better all the time," he says.

untry music has been good for years. Merle Haggard was certainly somebody I respected and who influenced my career a lot. You can't get better than that. George Jones, the same thing. You look at those guys, and they've been playing it for years. It's not like the people today are discovering something new. We're just kind of carrying on something that's been around for a long time. And we're damn lucky to be here."[169]

George also has the respect of his peers in Nashville. According to Alan Jackson, "One person whose career I've always admired, and his music, too, is George Strait. Of course, he came out at a time when country wasn't as hot. I mean, if he came out new now, he'd be like everybody else—selling millions. But, what I mean was he's been just constant and he comes out with great records and it's just continually selling and filling up the seats out on the road. He doesn't really make any big waves. He just keeps coming out with great music. It's pretty incredible to still have Number One records and selling Gold and Platinum like he is."[170]

Tracy Byrd says, "I never was one to get autographs or anything like that when I was a fan. But I'd have to say that George Strait would be the one. If I had to wait in line [at Fan Fair], I'd wait on him!"[171]

Like the character of Dusty, whom he portrayed in *Pure Country,* does George miss playing music in little honky-tonks and nightclubs? According to him, "No, I don't really miss them. I had fun then, but I have just as much fun doing the concerts I'm doing especially at the pace I'm doing them now. I really enjoy working more now than I did when I was working so much. I really got in a rut for a while. You get to the point where you're just like a machine, a robot. You go through the emotions of singing the songs, you go back to the bus, you go back to the hotel or you go on down the road to the next date. I wasn't getting off on that at all. It wasn't until I slowed down and it got to an easier, normal pace that I really enjoyed going out there and doing a show."[172]

If one was to stack up all of the George Strait albums, while there is a certain consistency, there has also been a constant change as well. "I think you can see a lot of changes," he points out, "especially when you take that first album [*Strait Country*] and listen to it, then listen to the last one [*Blue Clear Sky*]. My voice has matured more. Certainly I'm more confident than back then. I was pretty intimidated going into the studio the first time and playing with those guys. I'm sure that's the way it is in most people's careers. You become more confident in your situation. I think I'm singing better than I ever have. I'm still fired up."[173]

Fired up is right! From the catchy magnetism of "Unwound," through the fun of "All My Ex's Live in Texas," to the cinematic excitement of "Heartland," right up to the crisp clean beauty of "Blue Clear Sky," George Strait has had one of the most outrageously successful careers in the history of country music. Thankfully, this isn't the end of the George Strait saga; in reality it is just the beginning of a career that is destined to be remembered as fondly as that of his idol Bob Wills. George is here for the long run, and straight at the top of the country charts is right where he is destined to reign. As long as people still love the Texas sound of country music, there will be a singing, guitar-playing hero by the name of George Strait.

Chapter Fifteen

*"One Step At A Time—
An Epilogue"*

In the late 1990's, George Strait has time after time proven himself as county music's biggest selling and most enduring elder statesman. Number One hit songs, brand new multi-Platinum albums, sold-out shows, and record-breaking success with music awards, fan enthusiasm, and radio airplay, has kept his popularity unwaveringly strong.

By 1999 the album *Strait Out Of The Box* has sold in excess of five million copies, making it the biggest selling CD boxed set in the history of country music. George's *Strait Out Of The Box* is now ranked as one of the three biggest selling boxed sets ever released. (He is tied with Led Zeppelin, and surpassed only by Bruce Springsteen at this point).

As with all fads, from 1996 to 1998, Nashville had started to note that some of the luster had begun to fade from country music's early '90's boom. Sales figures and concert attendance records for several performers had topped off, and in many cases—had fallen. However, for George Strait, it seems that his time in the winner's circle has only just begun.

In 1996 alone, he won a total of three Country Music Association Awards, more than he has walked away with in any other single year. That same year his concert performances broke ticket sales records previously held by Hank WIlliams Sr., and Elvis Presley. He also broke several records which were previously set by himself!

When his 1997 album, *Carrying Your Love With Me* was released, George's legion of fans were thrilled to discover it to be one of the most satisfying and popular LP's of his career. Not only did the album hit Number One on *Billboard* magazine's charts, but it has gone on to sell well over three million copies. Produced by George and Tony Brown, Strait's natural instincts for his song selections on this release has again proven impeccable. From the catchy title cut, to the sentimental "The Nerve," to the effervescent swing sound of "That's Me (Every Chance I Get)," it has garnered a handful of awards, including the Country Music Association's trophy as 1997's Album Of The Year, in addition to the honor of George being declared their Male Vocalist Of The Year.

With regard to selecting songs for the *Carrying Your Love With Me* album, George explains, "The melody is real important to me. I feel like that's the thing that catches most people's ears first of all. Then I listen for the lyrics. Other than that, there's no one thing that I listen for in a song. It's just that I know it when it hits me, and that's the way it happens. You've got to be pleased with your work because you're the one who has to live with it, and I like this album. I just have to go in with the thought that I have to pick the best songs I can, and we usually find some great new song and a few that are old or sound like they are."

According to George's co-producer, Tony Brown, "George listens really close for songs. When a song shows up at the last minute that he likes he just puts his head phones on and goes in and learns the song. [The song]

'Blue Clear Sky' showed up on the morning of the last day we were recording that album. When it came in he loved it, and it took him about 30 minutes to learn. Then he went into the studio and recorded it. He's like an actor learning lines: he's a fast learner. If it's not right he'll go back in and study a little more and nail it to the wall."

With regard to the album *Carrying Your Love With Me*, Brown says, "The Dean Dillon/Gary Nicholson tune that's on the album, 'A Real Good Place To Start," is a real cool tune. Dean and Gary wrote all night long the night before they brought it to us—they knew me and George always meet every morning in his office here [in Nashville, Tennessee], so there we were, and Dean comes walking in and says, 'Hey George, I got one for you can I play it?' And, they did, and it was a really good song, and we cut it that day."

Also included on the *Carrying Your Love With Me* album is George's poignant version of Vern Gosdin's classic, "Today My World Slipped Away." As Brown so accurately describes Strait's interpretation of the song, "He just kills it." Another song on the album, "The Nerve," written by Bobby Braddock, Brown exclaims is "Braddock at his best!"

Seconding that opinion of "The Nerve," Strait adds, "What a neat song—it just blew me away! Where does this guy come up with such different lyrics that are so well thought out? I mean, his lyrics have so much structure and meaning, and they really tell a great story."

On this totally satisfying album of modern classics, George does a tiny bit of stylistic stretching out. Strait rarely uses a string sections on any of his songs, however it just seemed like the finishing touch when it came time to record the Jackson Leap song "She'll Leave You With A Smile."

"Why not?" asks George. "Just listen to it . . . the strings really set it off! There's no reason not to use them when a song calls for it."

In addition to the two Country Music Association awards that George won, during 1997 he also won an American Music Award in the category of Favorite Country Album for *Clear Blue Sky,* and the Academy Of Country Music declared him their Top Male Vocalist, as well as saluting *Clear Blue Sky* as their Album Of The Year.

When George's 23rd album, *One Step At A Time,* was released, he repeated his alchemy for picking hits. This 1998 Number One album continues George's hot streak on the charts, and in the hearts of his fans. The album's highlights include Jim Lauderdale's winning Top Ten composition "We Really Shouldn't Be Doing This," the catchy ode to love in Texas—"Remember The Alamo," and the brilliant honky tonk glow of "Neon Row." True to form, it instantly became a Platinum-selling success.

George's winning association with co-producer Tony Brown continues to be one of the most successful associations in all of country music. In addition to working with Strait, Brown is also the producer of 1990's hit albums by the likes of Trisha Yearwood and of Vince Gill—amongst others. Comparing Yearwood's wide stylistic style to Strait's tried and true formula, Brown claims, "Trisha is constantly pushing the envelope, and her music is more complex. One song will be very contemporary, one song may be folky, one song may be more rock, or more traditional—where George sort of does what he does. The sessions happen very quickly with George. We go in with the same musicians for the most part. They all know what he loves. I mean, by the first or second take we have it, because they become his band—the session players do. His sessions are really probably the easiest sessions that I do as far as things happening very quickly."

What is the reason for George Strait's consistent success in a business which seems to be constantly changing? According to Tony Brown, "George's music is honest. He never tries to follow any trends happening in country music. He just does what he does. He genuinely loves it. He loves the old guys, which is why we always try to do at least one remake. When we listen to the old records, I'll say 'Let's make it sound like this' and the smile on his face tells you that he loves country music. I know that sounds like a cliché, but he really does. I love working with him . . . I hope I can work with him for a long time."

Following the ebb and flow that occurs in the country music business, George finds that maintaining an even keel at all times is his formula for success. When he was recently asked what he thought about all of the changes that country music has experienced lately, he claims, "I think it's in a pretty healthy state. If you'll look at country music's history, it kind of has a way of taking care of itself and always seems to come back around to its roots." George, of course, never has to come back to his roots, because he never strays far from them.

In 1998, when the nominations for the 32nd annual Country Music Association Awards were announced, George Strait was nominated for five of the top trophies, including Entertainer Of The Year, Male Vocalist Of The Year, Album Of The Year (*One Step At A Time*), Single Of The Year ("I Just Want To Dance With You"), and Music Video Of The Year ("Carrying Your Love With Me"). These nominations made CMA history, ranking George as the most nominated country star ever to be honored by the CMA's, breaking a record previously held by Merle Haggard.

In his typically modest fashion, Strait proclaimed, "This is a great honor and I'm proud to hear about both the nominations and the record. I've been thrilled at each and every nomination I've ever received in my career. It always feels good to be recognized." When the awards were handed out on September 23, 1998, George was again named Male Vocalist Of The Year.

"I've gone through some years when the awards haven't come, so for me to pick up another one is real exciting. It's still an honor to be nominated and know that people appreciate what you do," he proclaimed.

After 23 albums, George Strait is genuinely startled to find himself listed as being an idol of some of today's hottest new country stars. According to him, "It kinda surprised me when I first started hearing how I had been an influence on some of the new guys in country music today. Then I started thinking about it, and although I wasn't trying to influence anybody, I realized that they were just looking at me like I had looked up to folks like Merle Haggard, George Jones and Bob Wills. It's a real honor to be in a similar situation."

What does the future hold for George Strait? According to him, "I'm just going to keep on trying to cut the best records I can." With regard to his concert touring schedule, he claims, "I want my fans to know that as long as they're going to keep coming to my shows that I'm going to keep coming out there and doing them. When I'm off, I have my other life, my own life, that I choose to live. I have my friends in Texas that don't have anything to do with the music business. And it's fun doing everything I can with my son, because he's into a lot of things. I play a lot of golf, I hunt and fish and I still rope a bit. I'm fortunate right now to have the time to do all the things that I really want to do—and enjoy myself."

When it comes time to tally the most successful country acts of the Twentieth Century, the name of George Strait is bound to be at the top of the list. Never wavering from his convictions, or the enjoyment he derives out of producing some of the most pleasing, and award-winning country music ever recorded, it seems that he has only just begun. If ever there was a George Strait formula for success, it would assuredly be: do the best you can—every chance you get, and take it "One Step At A Time."

George Strait Discography

Albums:

1. *Strait Country*
   (MCA Records/September 1981)

   —Produced by Blake Mevis

   (1) "Unwound"
       (Dean Dillon, Frank Dycus)

   (2) "Honky Tonk Down Stairs"
       (Dallas Frazier)

   (3) "Blame it on Mexico"
       (Darryl Staedtler)

   (4) "If You're Thinking You Want a Stranger"
       (Blake Mevis, David Wills)

   (5) "I Get Along with You"
       (Dean Dillon, Frank Dycus, Murray F. Cannon,
        Raleigh Squires, Jimmy Darrell)

(6) "Down and Out"
(Dean Dillon, Frank Dycus)

(7) "Friday Night Fever"
(Blake Mevis, Dean Dillon, Frank Dycus)

(8) "Every Time You Throw Dirt on Her (You Lose a Little Ground)"
(Michael Garvin, Tom Shapiro)

(9) "She's Playing Hell Trying to Get Me to Heaven"
(Dean Dillon, Charles Quillen, David Wills)

(10) "Her Goodbye Hit Me in the Heart"
(Dean Dillon, Frank Dycus)

2. *Strait from the Heart*
(MCA Records/June 1982)

—Produced by Blake Mevis

(1) "Fool Hearted Memory"
(Byron Hill, Alan R. Mevis)

(2) "Honky Tonk Crazy"
(Frank Dycus, Dean Dillon)

(3) "The Only Thing I Have Left"
(Clay Blaker)

(4) "The Steal of the Night"
(Bill Shore, David Wills, Alan R. Mevis)

(5) "I Can't See Texas from Here"
(George Strait)

(6) "Marina Del Rey"
(Dean Dillon, Frank Dycus)

(7) "Lover in Disguise"
(Alan R. Mevis, Jim Dowell)

(8) "Heartbroke"
(Guy C. Clark)

(9) "Amarillo by Morning"
(Terry Stafford, P. Fraser)

(10) "A Fire I Can't Put Out"
(Darryl Staedtler)

3. *Right or Wrong*
(MCA Records/October 1983)

—Produced by Ray Baker

(1) "You Look So Good in Love"
(Rory Bourke, Glen Ballard, Kerry Chater)

(2) "Right or Wrong"
(Arthur L. Sizemore, Haven Gillespie, Paul
Biese)

(3) "A Little Heaven's Rubbing Off on Me"
(John Scott Sherrill, Gene Dobbins)

(4) "80 Proof Bottle of Tear Stopper"
(Darryl Staedtler)

(5) "Every Time It Rains (Lord Don't It Pour)"
(Keith Stegall, Charlie Craig)

(6) "You're the Cloud I'm On (When I'm High)"
(Ronnie Rogers)

(7) "Let's Fall to Pieces Together"
(Dickey Lee, Tommy Rocco, Johnny Russell)

(8) "I'm Satisfied with You"
(Fred Rose)

(9) "Our Paths May Never Cross"
(Merle Haggard)

(10) "Fifteen Years Going Up (And One Night
Coming Down)"
(Peggy Forman)

4. ***Does Fort Worth Ever Cross Your Mind***
(MCA Records/September 1984)

—Produced by Jimmy Bowen and George Strait

(1) "Does Fort Worth Ever Cross Your Mind"
(Sanger D. Shafer, Darlene Shafer)

(2) "Any Old Time"
(Jeff Dayton, Katherine Elizabeth Nicoll)

(3) "I Need Someone Like Me"
(Sanger D. Shafer)

(4) "You're Dancin' This Dance All Wrong"
(John Porter McMeans, Ron Moore)

(5) "Honky Tonk Saturday Night"
(Sanger D. Shafer)

(6) "I Should Have Watched That First Step"
(Wayne Kemp)

(7) "Love Comes from the Other Side of Town"
(Fred J. Freiling)

(8) "The Cowboy Rides Away"
(Sonny Throckmorton, Casey Kelly)

(9) "What Did You Expect Me to Do"
    (Sanger D. Shafer)

(10) "The Fireman"
     (Mack Vickery, Wayne Kemp)

5. *George Strait: Greatest Hits*
   (MCA Records / March 1985)

   —Produced by Blake Mevis

   (except for) * Produced by Ray Baker

   (1) "Unwound"
       (Dean Dillon, Frank Dycus)

   (2) "Down and Out"
       (Dean Dillon, Frank Dycus)

   (3) "If You're Thinking You Want a Stranger
       (There's One Coming Home)"
       (Blake Mevis, David Wills)

   (4) "Fool Hearted Memory"
       (Byron Hill, Alan R. Mevis)

   (5) "Marina Del Rey"
       (Dean Dillon, Frank Dycus)

   (6) "Amarillo by Morning"
       (Terry Stafford, Paul Fraser)

   (7) "A Fire I Can't Put Out"
       (Darryl Staedtler)

   (8) "You Look So Good in Love"*
       (Rory Bourke, Glen Ballard, Kerry Chater)

   (9) "Right or Wrong"*
       (Arthur L. Sizemore, Haven Gillespie, Paul
       Biese)

(10) "Let's Fall to Pieces Together"*
     (Dickey Lee, Tommy Rocco, Johnny Russell)

6. *Something Special*
   (MCA Records/September 1985)

   —Produced by Jimmy Bowen and George Strait

   (1) "You're Something Special to Me"
       (David Anthony)

   (2) "Last Time the First Time"
       (Robert N. Kelly)

   (3) "Haven't You Heard"
       (Red Lane, Wayne Kemp)

   (4) "In Too Deep"
       (Jerry Max Lane, Erv Woolsey)

   (5) "Blue Is Not a Word"
       (Jo-el Sonnier, Judy Ball)

   (6) "You Sure Got This Ol' Redneck Feelin' Blue"
       (Dean Dillon, Buzz Rabin)

   (7) "The Chair"
       (Hank Cochran, Dean Dillon)

   (8) "Dance Time in Texas"
       (Peter Rowan)

   (9) "Lefty's Gone"
       (Sanger D. Shafer)

   (10) "I've Seen That Look on Me (A Thousand
        Times)"
        (Harlan Howard, Shirl Milete)

7. **#7**

   (MCA Records/May 1986)

   —Produced by Jimmy Bowen and George Strait

   (1) "Deep Water"
       (Fred Rose)

   (2) "Nobody in His Right Mind Would've Left Her"
       (Dean Dillon)

   (3) "Rhythm of the Road"
       (Dan McCoy)

   (4) "I'm Never Gonna Let You Go"
       (Clay Blaker)

   (5) "You Still Get to Me"
       (Dan McCoy)

   (6) "Stranger Things Have Happened"
       (David Chamberlain)

   (7) "It Ain't Cool to Be Crazy about You"
       (Dean Dillon, Royce Porter)

   (8) "Why'd You Go and Break My Heart"
       (David Anthony)

   (9) "My Old Flame Is Burnin' Another Honky Tonk
       Down"
       (Mack Vickery, Wayne Kemp, Bobby Borchers)

   (10) "Cow Town"
        (Hal Burns, Tex Ritter)

8. *Merry Christmas Strait to You*
(MCA Records/September 1986)

—Produced by Jimmy Bowen and George Strait

(1) "White Christmas"
(Irving Berlin)

(2) "There's a New Kid in Town"
(Curly Putman, Don Cook, Keith Whitley)

(3) "Winter Wonderland"
(Felix Bernard, Dick Smith)

(4) "Merry Christmas Strait to You"
(Bob Kelly)

(5) "Away in a Manger"
(Traditional/Arrangement: George Strait)

(6) "For Christ's Sake, It's Christmas"
(Hank Cochran, Dean Dillon)

(7) "Frosty the Snowman"
(Steve Nelson, Jack Rawlins)

(8) "When It's Christmas Time in Texas"
(Benny McArthur)

(9) "Santa Claus Is Coming to Town"
(J. Fred Coots, Haven Gillespie)

(10) "What a Merry Christmas This Could Be"
(Hank Cochran, Harlan Howard)

9. *Ocean Front Property*
   (MCA Records/January 1982

   —Produced by Jimmy Bowen and George Strait

   (1) "All My Ex's Live in Texas"
       (Sanger D. Shafer, Lyndia J. Shafer)

   (2) "Someone's Walkin' Around Upstairs"
       (David Anthony, Paul A. Maloy)

   (3) "Am I Blue"
       (David Chamberlain)

   (4) "Ocean Front Property"
       (Dean Dillon, Hank Cochran, Royce Porter)

   (5) "Hot Burning Flames"
       (Hank Cochran, Mack Vickery, Wayne Kemp)

   (6) "Without You Here"
       (Dean Dillon, Royce Porter)

   (7) "My Heart Won't Wander Very Far from You"
       (Annette Cotter, Buddy Carvalhe)

   (8) "Second Chances"
       (Sanger D. Shafer, Tommy Collins)

   (9) "You Can't Buy Your Way Out of the Blues"
       (Larry Cordle, Mike Anthony)

   (10) "I'm All Behind You Now"
        (Dean Dillon)

10. *George Strait: Greatest Hits Volume Two*
(MCA Records/September 1987)

—Produced by Jimmy Bowen and George Strait

(1) "Does Fort Worth Ever Cross Your Mind"
(Sanger D. Shafer, Darlene Shafer)

(2) "The Cowboy Rides Away"
(Sonny Throckmorton, Casey Kelly)

(3) "The Fireman"
(Mack Vickery, Wayne Kemp)

(4) "The Chair"
(Hank Cochran, Dean Dillon)

(5) "You're Something Special to Me"
(David Anthony)

(6) "Nobody in His Right Mind Would've Left
Her"
(Dean Dillon)

(7) "It Ain't Cool to Be Crazy about You"
(Dean Dillon, Royce Porter)

(8) "Ocean Front Property"
(Dean Dillon, Hank Cochran, Royce Porter)

(9) "All My Ex's Live in Texas"
(Sanger D. Shafer, Lyndia J. Shafer)

(10) "Am I Blue"
(David Chamberlain)

11. *If You Ain't Lovin', You Ain't Livin'*
   (MCA Records/February 1988)

   —Produced by Jimmy Bowen and George Strait

   (1) "If You Ain't Lovin' (You Ain't Livin')"
   (Tommy Collins)

   (2) "Under These Conditions"
   (Ronnie McDowell, Troy Seals, Joe Meador)

   (3) "Baby Blue"
   (Aaron Barker)

   (4) "Don't Mind If I Do"
   (Skip Ewing, Don Sampson)

   (5) "Bigger Man Than Me"
   (Curtis Wayne)

   (6) "Famous Last Words of a Fool"
   (Dean Dillon, Rex Huston)

   (7) "It's Too Late Now"
   (David Chamberlain)

   (8) "Is It That Time Again"
   (Dean Dillon, Buddy Cannon, Vern Gosdin)

   (9) "Let's Get Down to It"
   (L. David Lewis)

   (10) "Back to Bein' Me"
   (Dean Dillon, Hank Cochran)

12. *Beyond the Blue Neon*
   (MCA Records/February 1989)

   —Produced by Jimmy Bowen and George Strait

   (1) "Beyond the Blue Neon"
       (Paul Nelson, Larry Boone)

   (2) "Hollywood Squares"
       (Wayland Patton, Larry Cordle, Jeff Tanguay)

   (3) "Overnight Success"
       (Sanger D. Shafer)

   (4) "Ace in the Hole"
       (Dennis Adkins)

   (5) "Leavin's Been Comin' (For a Long, Long Time)"
       (Sonny Throckmorton, Dave Kirby, Joe Allen)

   (6) "Baby's Gotten Good at Goodbye"
       (Tony Martin, Troy Martin)

   (7) "What's Going On in Your World"
       (David Chamberlain, Royce Porter)

   (8) "Angel, Angelina"
       (L. David Lewis)

   (9) "Too Much of Too Little"
       (Curtis Wayne)

   (10) "Oh Me, Oh My Sweet Baby"
        (Michael Garvin, Tom Shapiro)

13. *Livin' It Up*
   (MCA Records/May 1990)

   —Produced by Jimmy Bowen and George Strait

   (1) "Someone Had to Teach You"
       (Harlan Howard)

   (2) "Heaven Must Be Wondering Where You Are"
       (L. David Lewis, David Chamberlain)

   (3) "I've Come to Expect It from You"
       (Dean Dillon, Buddy Cannon)

   (4) "Lonesome Rodeo Cowboy"
       (Clay Blaker)

   (5) "When You're a Man on Your Own"
       (Carl Perkins)

   (6) "Drinking Champagne"
       (Bill Mack)

   (7) "We're Supposed to Do That Now and Then"
       (Dean Dillon, David Anthony, Joe Royer)

   (8) "She Loves Me (She Don't Love You)"
       (Conway Twitty)

   (9) "Love Without End, Amen"
       (Aaron Barker)

   (10) "Stranger in My Arms"
        (Curtis Wayne)

14. *Chill of an Early Fall*
    (MCA Records/March 1991)

    —Produced by Jimmy Bowen and George Strait

    (1) "Chill of an Early Fall"
        (Green Daniel, Gretchen Peters)

    (2) "I've Convinced Everybody But Me"
        (L. David Lewis, Kim Williams, Buddy Cannon)

    (3) "If I Know Me"
        (Dean Dillon, Pam Belford)

    (4) "You Know Me Better Than That"
        (Tony Haselden, Anna Lisa Graham)

    (5) "Anything You Can Spare"
        (Harlan Howard)

    (6) "Home in San Antone"
        (Floyd Jenkins)

    (7) "Lovesick Blues"
        (Irving Mills, Cliff Friend)

    (8) "Milk Cow Blues"
        (Kokomo Arnold)

    (9) "Her Only Bad Habit Is Me"
        (Harlan Howard, Don Cook)

    (10) "Is It Already Time"
        (Aaron Barker)

15. *Ten Strait Hits*
(MCA Records/December 1991)

—Produced by Jimmy Bowen and George Strait

(1) "Famous Last Words of a Fool"
(Dean Dillon, Rex Huston)

(2) "Baby Blue"
(Aaron Barker)

(3) "If You Ain't Lovin' (You Ain't Livin')"
(Tommy Collins)

(4) "Baby's Gotten Good at Goodbye"
(Tony Martin, Troy Martin)

(5) "What's Going On in Your World"
(David Chamberlain, Royce Porter, Red
Steagall)

(6) "Ace in the Hole"
(Dennis Adkins)

(7) "Overnight Success"
(Sanger D. Shafer)

(8) "Love Without End, Amen"
(Aaron Barker)

(9) "Drinking Champagne"
(Bill Mack)

(10) "I've Come to Expect It from You"
(Dean Dillon, Buddy Cannon)

16. *Holding My Own*
(MCA Records/April 1992)

—Produced by Jimmy Bowen and George Strait

(1) "You're Right I'm Wrong"
(Marty Stuart, Wayne Perry)

(2) "Holding My Own"
(Dean Dillon, Pamela Belford)

(3) "Gone as a Girl Can Get"
(Jerry Max Lane)

(4) "So Much Like My Dad"
(Chips Moman, Bobby Emmons)

(5) "Trains Make Me Lonesome"
(Paul Overstreet, Thom Schuyler)

(6) "All of Me (Loves All of You)"
(Kim Williams, L. David Lewis, Monty Holmes)

(7) "Wonderland of Love"
(Curtis Wayne)

(8) "Faults and All"
(Carl Perkins)

(9) "It's Alright with Me"
(Jackson Leap)

(10) "Here We Go Again"
(Russell Steagall, Don Lanier)

17. *Pure Country*
(MCA Records/September 1992)

—Produced by Tony Brown and George Strait

(1) "Heartland"
(Steve Dorff, John Bettis)

(2) "Baby Your Baby"
(Phil Thomas, Hal Newman)

(3) "I Cross My Heart"
(Steve Dorff, Eric Kaz)

(4) "When Did You Stop Loving Me"
(Monty Holmes, Donny Kees)

(5) "She Lays It All on the Line"
(Clay Blaker)

(6) "Overnight Male"
(Kim Williams, Ron Harbin, Richard Fagan)

(7) "Last in Love"
(J. D. Souther, Glenn Frey)

(8) "Thoughts of a Fool"
(Mel Tillis, Wayne P. Walker)

(9) "The King of Broken Hearts"
(Jim Lauderdale)

(10) "Where the Sidewalk Ends"
(Jim Lauderdale, John Leventhal)

(11) "Heartland (Main Title Sequence)" [with
George Strait, Jr.]
(Steve Dorff, John Bettis)

18. ***Easy Come, Easy Go***
(MCA Records/September 1993)

—Produced by Tony Brown and George Strait

(1) "Stay Out of My Arms"
(Jim Lauderdale)

(2) "Just Look at Me"
(Curtis Wayne, Gerald Smith)

(3) "Easy Come, Easy Go"
(Aaron Barker, Dean Dillon)

(4) "I'd Like to Have That One Back"
(Bill Shore, Rick West, Aaron Barker)

(5) "Lovebug"
(Curtis Wayne, Wayne Kemp)

(6) "I Wasn't Fooling Around"
(Jim Lauderdale, John Leventhal)

(7) "Without Me Around"
(Dean Dillon, John Northrup)

(8) "The Man in Love with You"
(Steve Dorff, Gary Harju)

(9) "That's Where My Baby Feels at Home"
(Wayne Kemp, Curtis Wayne, Faron Young)

(10) "We Must Be Loving Right"
(Roger Brown, Clay Blaker)

19. *Lead On*
    (MCA Records/November 1994)

    —Produced by Tony Brown and George Strait

    (1) "You Can't Make a Heart Love Somebody"
        (Steve Clark, Johnny MacRae)

    (2) "Adalida"
        (Mike Geiger, Woody Mullis, Michael
          Huffman)

    (3) "I Met a Friend of Yours Today"
        (Wayland Holyfield, Bob McDill)

    (4) "Nobody Has to Get Hurt"
        (Jim Lauderdale, Terry A. McBride)

    (5) "Down Louisiana Way"
        (Aaron Barker, Donny Kees, Sanger D. Shafer)

    (6) "Lead On"
        (Dean Dillon, Teddy Gentry)

    (7) "What Am I Waiting For"
        (Jim Lauderdale)

    (8) "The Big One"
        (Gerry House, Devon O'Day)

    (9) "I'll Always Be Loving You"
        (Aaron Barker, Donny Kees, Sanger D. Shafer)

    (10) "No One But You"
         (Max D. Barnes)

20. *Strait Out of the Box*
    (MCA Records/September 1995)

    —Produced by various producers including Don
        Daily, Blake Mevis, Ray Baker, Jimmy
        Bowen, George Strait, Joe Bob Barnhill, Tony
        Brown, Ray Benson, Phil Ramone, Hank
        Cataneo

Disk One:

(1) "I Just Can't Go On Dying Like This"
    (George Strait)

(2) "(That Don't Change) The Way I Feel about
    You"
    (George Strait)

(3) "I Don't Want to Talk It Over Anymore"
    (George Strait)

(4) "Unwound"
    (Dean Dillon, Frank Dycus)

(5) "Blame it on Mexico"
    (Darryl Staedtler)

(6) "Her Goodbye Hit Me in the Heart"
    (Dean Dillon, Frank Dycus)

(7) "If You're Thinking You Want a Stranger
    (There's One Coming Home)"
    (Blake Mevis, David Wills)

(8) "Any Old Love Won't Do"
    (Dean Dillon, Frank Dycus)

(9) "Fool Hearted Memory"
    (Byron Hill, Alan R. Mevis)

(10) "Marina Del Rey"
     (Dean Dillon, Frank Dycus)

(11) "I Can't See Texas from Here"
     (George Strait)

(12) "Heartbroke"
     (Guy C. Clark)

(13) "What Would Your Memories Do"
     (Hank Cochran, Dean Dillon)

(14) "Amarillo by Morning"
     (Terry Stafford, Paul Fraser)

(15) "I Thought I Heard You Calling My Name"
     (Lee Emerson)

(16) "A Fire I Can't Put Out"
     (Darryl Staedtler)

(17) "You Look So Good in Love"
     (Rory Bourke, Glen Ballard, Kerry Chater)

(18) "80 Proof Bottle of Tear Stopper"
     (Darryl Staedtler)

Disk Two:

(1) "Right or Wrong"
    (Arthur L. Sizemore, Haven Gillespie, Paul
    Biese)

(2) "Let's Fall to Pieces Together"
    (Dickey Lee, Tommy Rocco, Johnny Russell)

(3) "Does Fort Worth Ever Cross Your Mind"
    (Sanger D. Shafer, Darlene Shafer)

(4) "The Cowboy Rides Away"
    (Sonny Throckmorton, Casey Kelly)

(5) "The Fireman"
     (Mack Vickery, Wayne Kemp)

(6) "The Chair"
     (Hank Cochran, Dean Dillon)

(7) "You're Something Special to Me"
     (David Anthony)

(8) "Haven't You Heard"
     (Red Lane, Wayne Kemp)

(9) "In Too Deep"
     (Jerry Max Lane, Erv Woolsey)

(10) "Lefty's Gone"
      (Sanger D. Shafer)

(11) "Nobody in His Right Mind Would've Left
      Her"
      (Dean Dillon)

(12) "In Ain't Cool to Be Crazy about You"
      (Dean Dillon, Royce Porter)

(13) "Ocean Front Property"
      (Dean Dillon, Hank Cochran, Royce Porter)

(14) "Rhythm of the Road"
      (Dan McCoy)

(15) "Six Pack to Go" [with Hank Thompson]
      (J. Lowe, Hank Thompson, D. Hart)

(16) "All My Ex's Live in Texas"
      (Sanger D. Shafer, Lyndia J. Shafer)

(17) "Am I Blue"
      (David Chamberlain)

(18) "Famous Last Words of a Fool"
      (Dean Dillon)

Disk Three:

(1) "Baby Blue"
(Aaron Barker)

(2) "If You Ain't Lovin' (You Ain't Livin')"
(Tommy Collins)

(3) "Baby's Gotten Good at Goodbye"
(Tony Martin, Troy Martin)

(4) "Bigger Man Than Me"
(Curtis Wayne)

(5) "Hollywood Squares"
(Wayland Patton, Larry Cordle, Jeff Tanguay)

(6) "What's Going On in Your Mind"
(David Chamberlain, Royce Porter, Red
Steagall)

(7) "Ace in the Hole"
(Dennis Adkins)

(8) "Love Without End, Amen"
(Aaron Barker)

(9) "Drinking Champagne"
(Bill Mack)

(10) "I've Come to Expect It from You"
(Dean Dillon, Buddy Cannon)

(11) "If I Know Me"
(Dean Dillon, Pam Melford)

(12) "You Know Me Better Than That"
(Tony Haselden, Anna Lisa Graham)

(13) "The Chill of an Early Fall"
(Green Daniel, Gretchen Peters)

(14) "Lovesick Blues"
(Irving Mills, Cliff Friend)

(15) "Milk Cow Blues"
(Kokomo Arnold)

(16) "Gone as a Girl Can Get"
(Jerry Max Lane)

(17) "So Much Like My Dad"
(Chips Moman, Bobby Emmons)

(18) "Trains Make Me Lonesome"
(Paul Overstreet, Thom Schuyler)

Disk Four:

(1) "Wonderland of Love"
(Curtis Wayne)

(2) "I Cross My Heart"
(Steve Dorff, Eric Kaz)

(3) "Heartland"
(Steve Dorff, John Bettis)

(4) "When Did You Stop Loving Me"
(Monty Holmes, Donny Kees)

(5) "Overnight Male"
(Kim Williams, Ron Harbin, Richard Fagan)

(6) "The King of Broken Hearts"
(Jim Lauderdale)

(7) "Where the Sidewalk Ends"
(Jim Lauderdale, John Leventhal)

(8) "Easy Come, Easy Go"
(Aaron Barker, Dean Dillon)

(9) "I'd Like to Have That One Back"
(Bill Shore, Rick West, Aaron Barker)

(10) "Lovebug"
(Curtis Wayne, Wayne Kemp)

(11) "The Man in Love with You"
(Steve Dorff, Gary Harju)

(12) "Just Look at Me"
(Curtis Wayne, Gerald Smith)

(13) "Stay Out of My Arms"
(Jim Lauderdale)

(14) "Big Ball's in Cowtown" [with Asleep at the Wheel]
(Hoyle Nix)

(15) "The Big One"
(Gerry House, Devon O'Day)

(16) "Fly Me to the Moon" [with Frank Sinatra]
(Bart Howard)

(17) "Check Yes or No"
(Danny M. Wells, Dana Hunt Oglesby)

(18) "I Know She Still Loves Me"
(Aaron Barker, Monty Holmes)

21. *Blue Clear Sky*
(MCA Records/April 1996)

—Produced by Tony Brown and George Strait

(1) "Blue Clear Sky"
(Mark D. Sanders, John Jarrard, Bob DiPiero)

    (2) "Carried Away"
        (Steve Bogard, Jeff Stevens)

    (3) "Rockin' in the Arms of Your Memory"
        (Dean Dillon, Norro Wilson)

    (4) "She Knows When You're on My Mind"
        (Wayne Kemp, Mack Vickery)

    (5) "I Ain't Never Seen No One Like You"
        (Roger Springer, Bruce Bouton, Mark
          Chesnutt)

    (6) "I Can Still Make Cheyenne"
        (Aaron Barker, Erv Woolsey)

    (7) "King of the Mountain"
        (Paul Nelson, Larry Boone)

    (8) "Do the Right Thing"
        (Jim Lauderdale, Gary Nicholson)

    (9) "I'd Just as Soon Go"
        (Dean Dillon, Aaron Barker)

    (10) "Need I Say More"
         (Clay Blaker, Roger Brown)

22. *Carrying Your Love With Me*
    (MCA Records/April 1997)

    —Produced by Tony Brown and George Strait

    (1) "Round About Way"
        (Steve Dean, Wil Nance)

    (2) "Carrying Your Love With Me"
        (Jeff Stevens, Steve Bogard)

(3) "One Night At A Time"
   (Roger Cook, Eddie Kilgallon, Earl Bud Lee)

(4) "She'll Leave You With A Smile"
   (Jackson Leap)

(5) "Won't You Come Home (And Talk To A
   Stranger)"
   (Wayne Kemp)

(6) "Today My World Slipped Away"
   (Mark Wright, Vern Gosdin)

(7) "I've Got A Funny Feeling"
   (Harlan Howard, Jackson Leap)

(8) "The Nerve"
   (Bobby Braddock)

(9) "That's Me (Every Chance I Get)"
   (Mark D. Sanders, Ed Hill)

(10) "A Real Good Place To Start"
   (Dean Dillon, Gary Nicholson)

23. *One Step At A Time*
   (MCA Records/April 1998)

   —Produced by Tony Brown and George Strait

(1) "I Just Want To Dance With You"
   (Roger Cook, John Prine)

(2) "One Step At A Time"
   (Earl Clark, Luke Reed)

(3) "True"
   (Marv Green, Jeff Stevens)

(4) "Remember The Alamo"
(Gordon Kennedy, Wayne Kilpatrick)

(5) "Maria"
(Robert Earl Keen, Jr.)

(6) "We Really Shouldn't Be Doing This Thing"
(Jim Lauderdale)

(7) "Why Not Now"
(Steve Bogard, Jeff Stevens)

(8) "That's The Breaks"
(Dean Dillon, Royce Porter)

(9) "Neon Row"
(Jimmy Jay, Donny Kees)

(10) "You Haven't Left Me Yet"
(Dana Hunt, Kent M. Robbins)

Sources

1,8,13,17,34,37,105,116,124,143,144,146,162,163,166,169, 172,173—*Blue Clear Sky* album review by Robert Baird, *New Country*, May 1996.

2,6,15,21,22,29,31,33,35,65, 79,96,126,128,138,140,141,148, 150—Liner Notes by Paul Kingsbury for *Strait Out of the Box*, MCA Records 1995.

3,7,20,23,28,32,44,49,74,86,90,91—"George Strait and the Ace in the Hole band Pick Up the Pieces Where Bob Wills Left Off" by Bob Allen, *Country Music*, September/ October 1988.

4,26,64,73,75,78,82,83,87,88,—"Strait Fever" by Bob Allen, *Country Music*, March/April 1990.

5,30,155,158,159,164—"George Strait: Why He Stays Private" by Mike Greenblat, *Modern Screen's Country Music*, July 1996.

9—"Tribute to the Music of Bob Wills and His Texas

Playboys," Liner Notes, *Asleep at the Wheel,* Liberty Records, 1993.

10,66,152,168—"George Strait: Country's Unassuming Superstar Would Rather Be Roping on the Ranch Than Rambling about Himself" by Curt Goettsch, *Country America,* May 1993.

11,16,18,19,48,62,95,123,127,154,167—"George Strait: The Enigmatic Cowboy" by Daniel Cooper, *The Journal of Country Music,* 1995.

12,38,72,77,84,85,89—"George Strait: *Blue Neon* May Be the Best Album the CMA's Newest 'Entertainer of the Year' Has Ever Done" by Deborah Evans Price, *Tune In,* November 1989.

14,27,63,71,92—"George Strait: A Quiet Texan Hangs His Hat on a Star" by Sandy Lovejoy, *Tune In,* December 1988.

24,76,101,113,161—"George Strait: I Almost Packed It In!" by Rex Rutkowski, *Modern Screen's Country Music Special,* January 1992.

25,43,50,51—"Not Even Waylon or Willie Bridle at George Strait's Ride to Country Music Stardom" written by Montgomery Brower & reported by Kent Demaret, *People,* 1985.

36—*Music City News,* 1981.

39,40,41,42—"Country Purists Fight Back" by David Gates, *Newsweek,* January 9, 1984.

45,137,151—"George Strait Invites You to His 25 #1 Hit Party" by Gerry Wood, *Country Weekly,* April 1995.

46,47—"On the Road with George Strait" by Bob Campbell, *Country Rhythms,* 1984.

52—" '85 CMA Awards: A Return to Tradition," *Music City News,* November 1985.

53,56,57,61,70—"All Cowboy, No Bull" by John Lomax III, *Country Song Roundup,* 1985.

54,55,59,60—"George Strait: The Man under the White Hat" by Patrick Carr, *Country Music,* 1986.

58—#7 album review by James Hunter, *Rolling Stone,* 1986.

67,68—Article by Gerry Wood, *Billboard,* 1988.

69—"Essential Collector: Country Video Library" by Rich Kienzle, *Country Music,* July 1990.

80,81,131—"Strait Toes a Straight Line to Success" by David Zimmerman, *USA Today,* August 17, 1990.

93—"George, Strait Ahead" by Alanna Nash, *Entertainment Weekly,* April 12, 1991.

94—"Chill of an Early Fall" record review by Bob Allen, *Country Music,* 1991.

97—"Holding My Own" record review by Geoffrey Himes. *Country Music,* May 1992.

98—"Holding My Own" record review by Ralph Novak, *People,* 1992.

99,100,156—"Strait Talk with George" by Mike Greenblatt, *Modern Screen's Country Music,* 1996.

102,103,115,125—*Country Hunks* by Mark Bego, Contemporary Books, Chicago, IL, 1994.

104,111—"Strait from the Heart" by Gerry Wood, *Country America,* July/August 1991.

106,112,132—"No Acting Lessons for George Strait before *Pure Country*" by Joe Edwards for Associated Press, *Cedar Rapids Gazette,* October 30, 1992.

107,108—"He's the New Elvis: Colonel Parker's Secret Plan for *Pure Country's* George Strait" *The Star,* 1992.

109,110,118,119—"On the Set of *Pure Country* with George Strait," *Chicago Country,* September/October 1992.

114,117,120,121,129,130—"George Strait: Screen Idol" by Michael McCall, *Country Music,* 1992.

122—"Crossing Over: Country Superstar George Strait Plays Something Very Close to, Well, George Strait" by Kevin Phinney, *Premiere,* November 1992.

133—*Pure Country* movie review by Ralph Novak, *People,* November 9, 1992.

134—*"Pure Country* Purely for George Strait Fans" movie review by Roger Ebert, *United Press Syndicate,* October 1992.

135—*Pure Country* album review by Bob Allen, *Country Music,* 1992.

136—"George Strait Returns to Form", *Country Spectacular,* 1992.

139—"George Strait: On the Road and More" by Tyler Michael, *Modern Screen's Country Music Special,* October 1993.

142—"Lead On" record review by Craig Peters, *Country-Beat* April 1995.

145,149,160,165—"For the Very First Time, He Talks about the Tragedy That Broke His Heart" by Gerry Wood, *Country Weekly,* November 14, 1995.

147—"Riding & Roping with George Strait" by Larry Holden, *Country Weekly,* July 25, 1995.

153—"George Strait Ropes & Relaxes at His Texas Ranch" by Gerry Wood, *Country Weekly,* March 21, 1995.

157—*Blue Clear Sky* album review by Robert Baird, *New Country,* May 1996.

170—*Alan Jackson: Gone Country* by Mark Bego, Taylor Publishing, Dallas, TX, 1996.

171—"Country Notes" column, Country Weekly, July 9, 1996.

Also Consulted

"ASCAP Picks 'I Swear,' " This Just In column, *Country Weekly,* October 1995.

Armstrong, Gene, "It's Strait to the Audience's Heart", *Arizona Daily Star,* October 10, 1992.

"Back in the Saddle", *Country America,* July/August 1995.

Biracree, Tom, *The Country Music Almanac,* Prentice Hall Publishers, New York, NY, 1993.

Browne, David, "Big Country," *Entertainment Weekly,* March 20, 1992.

"Country Notes" column, *Country Weekly,* July 2, 1996.

Elvis Presley: The King of Rock & Roll—The Complete '50s Masters, album's liner notes.

Flippo, Chet, "Inside Country Music," *People,* May 21, 1984.

"George Strait: Fact File," *CountryBeat,* April 1995.

"George Strait Talks Turkey & Spanish Rice," *Country Weekly,* January 9, 1996.

"George Strait's Dog On The Run," This Just In column, *Country Weekly,* January 30, 1996.

Gubernick, Lisa and Newcomb, Peter, "Led Zeppelin Meets Roy Rogers . . . Country Conquers Rock/The Wal-mart School of Music," *Forbes,* March 2, 1992.

Holden, Larry, "George Strait Throws a Labor Day Party," *Country Weekly,* October 10, 1995.

"Howdy!" *Strait-A-Way,* May 1995.

Jinkins, Shirley, "What Is It about Texas & Country Music/ Texas Titan George Strait Is Still Country's Top Hat," *Country America,* October 1995.

Marymont, Mark, "Garth Leads in All-Time Country Album Sales," *Country Weekly,* May 6–31, 1996.

Maltin, Leonard, *TV Movies and Video Guide,* Signet Books, 1987.

"Nashville's Cats in Hats," *People,* March 30, 1992.

Parrish, Pam, "Strait Gives a Straightforward, Crowd-Pleasing Show, *Arizona Daily Star,* June 10, 1990.

Rees, Dafydd and Crampton, Luke, *Rock Movers & Shakers,* Billboard Books, New York, NY, 1991.

Rutkoski, Rex, "George Strait: No Rest for the Weary," *Modern Screen Yearbook #32,* 1992.

Skinner, M. Scott, "Crowd Liked Its Country Strait Up," *Arizona Daily Star,* March 6, 1989.

Skinner, M. Scott, "George Strait Is a Real Hero to His Fans," *Arizona Daily Star.*

Skinner, M. Scott, "Sold-Out TCC Audience Swings to No-Frills Strait," *Arizona Daily Star,* June 8, 1991.

Stanley, David, *The Elvis Encyclopedia,* Virgin Books, London, England, 1984.

"Strait from the Heart," *Starline Presents: Garth Brooks and Country Music's Hottest Stars,* 1991.

"Strait to the Trophy Case," This Just In column, *Country Weekly,* October 3, 1995.

Whitburn, Joel, *Top Pop: 1955–1982,* Record Research, Inc., Menomonee Falls, WI, 1983.

Woliver, Robbie, "George Strait Keeps His Daughter's Memory Alive," *Country Weekly,* February 6, 1996.

Wood, Gerry, "George Strait: Roping in a Herd of Hits," *Country Weekly,* September 19, 1995.

Wood, Gerry, "Three off the Best for Garth," *Country Weekly,* April 16, 1996.

About the Author

Mark Bego is a *New York Times* best-selling author with thirty-one books published and eight million books in print. He is the biggest selling biographer in the rock & roll and pop music field. His book *Bonnie Raitt: Just in the Nick of Time,* which chronicles Raitt's triumph over drugs and liquor, was published in 1995. Also published in 1995 was Bego's look at the life of Patsy Cline, *I Fall to Pieces: The Music and the Life of Patsy Cline.*

His reference book of ultra-fascinating facts and off-the-wall lists as well as biographies, *The Rock & Roll Almanac,* was published by Macmillan in 1996.

Mark has also written several other biographies of music industry celebrities. Among them are Barry Manilow, Michael Jackson, Whitney Houston, Cher, Bette Midler, and Aretha Franklin. His biggest selling biographies were 1984's *Michael!,* a biography of Michael Jackson, and *Madonna!.*

Bego just finished a book with David Stanley about rock & roll's most dysfunctional family called *Raised on the*

Rock: The Autobiography of Elvis Presley's Stepbrother. Currently, Bego and the Supremes' Mary Wilson are working on a music business mystery novel entitled *Motor City*.

Mark's writing has also appeared in several magazines including *People, US*, the *Star, Celebrity, Cosmopolitan, Penthouse, Billboard* and the *National Enquirer*. From 1983 to 1985 he was the editor-in-chief of *Modern Screen* magazine.

Mark Bego divides his time between New York City, Los Angeles and Tucson, Arizona.

CELEBRITY BIOGRAPHIES

GIFT BOOKS TO READ AND PASS ALONG